Wartime Poland, 1939–1945

Recent Titles in
Bibliographies and Indexes in World History

Wartime Poland, 1939–1945

A Select Annotated Bibliography of Books in English

WALTER OKONSKI

Bibliographies and Indexes in World History,
Number 45

GP

GREENWOOD PRESS
Westport, Connecticut • London

Library of Congress Cataloging-in-Publication Data

Okonski, Walter, 1935–
    Wartime Poland, 1939–1945 : a select annotated bibliography of
books in English / Walter Okonski.
        p.   cm.—(Bibliographies and indexes in world history, ISSN
0742–6852 ; no. 45)
    Includes indexes.
    ISBN 0–313–30004–6 (alk. paper)
    1. World War, 1939–1945—Poland—Bibliography. 2. Poland—
History—Occupation, 1939–1945—Bibliography. I. Title.
II. Series.
D765056   1997
[Z6207.W8]
016.94053'438—dc20   96—33027

British Library Cataloguing in Publication Data is available.

Library of Congress Catalog Card Number: 96–33027
ISBN: 0–313–30004–6
ISSN: 0742–6852

First published in 1997

Greenwood Press, 88 Post Road West, Westport, CT 06881
An imprint of Greenwood Publishing Group, Inc.

Printed in the United States of America

∞™

The paper used in this book complies with the
Permanent Paper Standard issued by the National
Information Standards Organization (Z39.48–1984).

10 9 8 7 6 5 4 3 2

To my wife, Maria, who has helped so much

CONTENTS

viii   Contents

INTRODUCTION

PURPOSE

The *Wartime Poland, 1939-1945* bibliography has been written
to serve as a quick source of information and useful guidance
for researchers who are interested in the subject but are
unfamiliar with the Polish language. It organizes and
annotates several hundred English-language monographs, books,
book chapters, and government documents.

BACKGROUND

Over the past decades wartime Poland has received much
attention of Anglo-American historians and other researchers.
Hundreds of books, memoirs, government documents, articles,
films, and a variety of other documentary materials have
appeared that deal with the Polish aspects of WW II. Interest
in this area has increased even more noticeably during the
last several years driven by dramatic political changes in
this country. Surprisingly, there has been to date no
progress in integrating this literary production, which
continues to grow, in one organized bibliographic coverage.
No bibliography was available to anyone who does not understand
Polish. Given the number of books published in English each
year, lack of a comprehensive bibliographic guide to this
copious material, and the identified reader interest, this
author was prompted to compile a selected annotated
bibliography of pertinent books on the subject. The *Wartime
Poland, 1939-1945* is a result of several years of extensive
literature review.

SCOPE

The bibliography, the first of its kind yet available in
this country, brings together over 350 significant English-
language monographs, books, book chapters, and government
documents published in the United States and elsewhere in the

years 1940-1996. Not definitive, it is aimed at
comprehensiveness in that it seeks to address virtually all
the main aspects of Poland's participation in the war
conflict: causes, course, military and political, and legal
and economic concerns. Inevitably, the emphasis is placed on
the social impact of the war: occupation, terror, the
Holocaust and other atrocities, as well as the Polish
question and war consequences. The work seeks to set the
addressed issues in a broader international context.

USERS

The bibliography is intended to be a practical reference
guide for the majority of researchers, especially those
dealing with the European aspects of WW II: history students
and teachers, historians, scholars, and journalists. While
written primarily with these categories of users in mind, it
still has many books that may attract attention of a wider
general audience. It is hoped it will also appeal to the
interests of WW II enthusiasts, those interested in military,
clandestine operations, and diplomatic activities. It
provides useful insights into some complex aspects of Polish
history and shows a gallery of historical figures that shaped
Poland's fate in the war years and immediately thereafter. In
fact, the bibliography is addressed to everyone who wishes to
know more, in a condensed form, about a variety of issues
concerning the subject.

MATERIAL AND SELECTION

A combined, computerized and manual search of major
bibliographic utilities (OCLC and RLIN), online public-access
catalog databases, bibliographies, book review publications,
abstract journals, and other reference sources was conducted
to locate pertinent materials dealing or linked with the
subject. For the purpose of this work, the following were not
considered: pamphlets/brochures, fiction, poetry, works of
artistic content, doctoral dissertations. Books in Polish
were evaluated only when they were translated or provided
English summaries. Inclusions were based on the quality
criteria: importance of authors and/or publishers, and
favorable reviews. As a result of this selection, the
bibliography offers works written by notable authors, each
one an acknowledged authority in his/her field. Some works
were included without regard to their scholarly merit. These
are popular accounts on various topical aspects chosen to
reach a wider readership.
A few items listed have not been available for evaluation
at the final phase of compiling. Such titles are presented
because the bibliographic citation suggests they might
provide useful contribution. These items are marked "N.A."
("not available").
Two extra features should further increase the practical
value of this reference tool. First, a recent re-examination
of OCLC and RLIN resources indicates that over 90% of the
inclusions are now available via these databases--useful
information for those who, guided by an annotation, will

choose to obtain a book through Inter Library Loan services.
Second, in recognition of the fact that with its resources
and retrieval facilities New York City attracts numerous U.S.
and European researchers, the collections of the three large
library systems--New York Public Library Research Libraries,
including its Slavonic and Jewish divisions, Mid-Manhattan
Library's History and Social Science divisions, and Brooklyn
Public Library--were searched for the items in this
bibliography. The New York Public Library and Mid-Manhattan
were found to contain most of the selections listed.

ARRANGEMENT

Examination of the Contents shows the organization of the
bibliography and points out just how extensively the subject
matter is covered. The material is divided into 9 groups,
further broken down into more specific topics. The
organization and terminology used resulted largely from the
leading topics of the items selected. Subdivisions were based
on the amount of material available on a given topic. A
minimum of 3-4 entries on each subdivision was decided to
give the user a good choice. The general reader should find
this quantity enough to satisfy his interest, and the
professional a sufficient basis from which to continue
further research. Under each subdivision books are arranged
alphabetically by authors. Each book received an entry number
and these numbers run consecutively throughout the
bibliography. Some of the books, because they cover various
issues, have been classified under more than one subgroup.
Following bibliographic citations are annotations, mostly
descriptive, though some include evaluative comments.
Annotations clarify the contents of books, titles if not
clear enough, convey authors' viewpoints, and, when
appropriate, some information about authors or their pro- and
anti-biases. Often, they draw attention to some particularly
useful or attractive features of the book. Finally, author,
title, and subject indexes are provided to facilitate access
to individual works *(Note that numbers in indexes refer to
entry numbers)*.

LIMITATIONS

Given its nature, the bibliography has several limitations.
First, it restricts entries to books and only to those
meeting the criteria. Second, no one will agree entirely with
the choices made or the space given to various topics. Some
scholars may believe that other books would supersede some of
the titles listed or that some titles have been omitted.
Still, as the bibliography is basically meant to serve
research purposes, an effort was made to select the works
that would meet the needs of the readership in mind. The
purpose was to provide these users with a guide of real
value. Yet another weak point is the limited number of
entries by Polish authors. Especially in Poland, a multitude
of in-scope works have appeared in English that would make
considerable contributions to the subject area. I was able to
evaluate only a fragment of this material. The present guide,

accordingly, cannot pretend to be exhaustive. Instead, it is
a selective survey of more important pertinent books.
Nevertheless, although it cannot satisfy every user's needs,
it does, at least, attempt to be as comprehensive in scope as
possible. It is presented in the belief that some
imperfections cannot spoil the main objective of opening up
the subject to a wider spectrum of readers for whom Polish
wartime history was until now something remote and
inaccessible. Finally, I believe that the concerns outlined
in this work will intensify Western interest in this broad
research area of growing importance and make researchers
aware of plenty of great new material now available and
awaiting their exploration particularly in Polish libraries
and archives. If the book achieves only that goal, it will
have been worthwhile.

BIBLIOGRAPHY

1

POLAND IN THE
TWENTIETH CENTURY

1a. GENERAL ACCOUNTS

1. Barnett, Clifford R. *Poland: Its People, Its Society, Its Culture*. New Haven, Conn.: HRAF Press, 1958. 470p., maps, bibl. (Survey of world cultures).
   The survey looks briefly at Poland's past but concentrates on the twentieth century, especially on the post-war period. The material is grouped under such headings as geography and population, religions, political system, government structure and the role of the Communist party, domestic and foreign trade, ethnic groups and languages, and art and intellectual expression.

2. Dziewanowski, M. K. *Poland in the Twentieth Century*. New York: Columbia University Press, 1977. 309p., bibl.
   In nine chapters, professor of history at Boston University describes and analyzes developments in Poland's history from the earliest times to the mid-1970s. The first two chapters summarize Polish history before 1914. The succeeding ones cover the period following World War One. The context of the German and Russian menace to Poland is extensively exposed. The book is written in a lively style and language and presents a balanced coverage of politics, economy, culture, education, and social issues of pre- and post-war Poland.

3. Griffith, William E. *The Ostpolitik of the Federal Republic of Germany*. Cambridge, Mass: MIT Press, 1978. 325p., bibl. (Center for International Studies in Communism, Revisionism, and Revolution, vol. 24).
   Examines the policies of West Germany toward its neighbors to the East, with special focus on all its treaties with them. The opening chapter traces the development of Ostpolitik from the Prussian attitudes toward Poland, Russia, and the Balkan states up to the partition of Germany following World War II. The remaining chapters present an analysis of the Bonn government's relations with the Soviet Union and East European countries.

4. Landau, Zbigniew, and Jerzy Tomaszewski. *The Polish
Economy in the Twentieth Century*. Translated from the Polish
by Wojciech Roszkowski. New York: St. Martin's Press, 1985.
345p., bibl.
   The authors cover the economic history of Poland from the
partition before WW I to 1980. They concentrate on population
changes, industrial development, agriculture, finance,
domestic trade, foreign economic relations, and living
conditions.

5. Leslie, R. F., et al., ed. *The History of Poland since
1863*. Cambridge; New York: Cambridge University Press, 1980.
494p., maps, bibl. (Soviet and East European Studies).
   "This work is an account of the evolution of Poland from
conditions of subjection to its reconstitution in 1918,
development in the years between the two World Wars, and
reorganization after 1944-45." (Publisher's note). This is a
condensation of the fuller histories the authors of the book
have previously written independently. A good balance among
political, social, intellectual, and economic history.
Contains a wealth of graphs, charts, and statistics to
support its authors' various conclusions.

6. Lundgreen-Nielsen, Kay. *The Polish Problem at the Paris
Peace Conference: A Study of the Policies of the Great Powers
and the Poles, 1918-1919*. Odense, Denmark: Odense University
Press, 1979. 603p., bibl. (Odense universitet. Studies in
History and Social Sciences, vol. 59\59). Originally
presented as the author's thesis, Odense, 1977.
   The Great Powers had to deal with many problems at the
Peace Conference, but the Polish question--the problem of
re-establishing the Polish State--was one of the most
important because the restoration of Poland concerned
relations with two former Great Powers, Germany and Russia.
Now in a weak position and not taking part in the Conference
and its decisions, they were expected to take again their
places among the Powers. The restoration of Poland was
accepted. This study concentrates on the Polish problem as
seen by both the Polish side and Great Powers at the various
phases of the Conference, as the Polish question demonstrated
the clashes of interests on several points between the
participants.

7. Rosenthal, Harry Kenneth. *German and Pole: National
Conflict and Modern Myth*. Gainesville: University Presses of
Florida, 1976. 175p., bibl. (A Florida State University Book
series).
   A historical survey of the German-Polish relations from the
end of the 19th century up to 1970s.

8. Schreiber, Hermann. *Teuton and Slav: The Struggle for
Central Europe*. Translated from the German edition by James
Cleugh. New York: Knopf, 1965. 392p., ill., portraits, maps,
bibl. Translation of *Land in Osten*.
   A historical outline of the relationships between the
Germanic and Slavic peoples throughout centuries up to the
present time. Written with the hope of "redressing the
nationalistic prejudices of their respective
historiographies" (Am Hist Rev). Unlike many German

historians, Schreiber attempts to relate the subject in an
impartial spirit and sees the Slavic contributions to the
civilization of the region as equal to the German.

9. Wandycz, Piotr Stefan. *Polish Diplomacy 1914-1945: Aims
and Achievements: A Lecture in English and Polish.* Edited
and prepared for publication by Keith Sword. London: Orbis
Books, 1988. 139p., plates, ill., portraits, bibl. (M.B.
Grabowski Memorial Lecture Series, 3). Published for the
School of Slavonic and East European Studies by Orbis Books.
Text in English and Polish.
   Published in the M.B. Grabowski Memorial Lecture Series,
this work traces Polish diplomatic history from World War I
to the end of World War II. Focus is on the main goals and
achievements of the Polish diplomacy of this period.

10. _____ . *The United States and Poland.* Boston: Harvard
Univ. Press, 1980. 465p., maps, bibl. (American Foreign
Policy Library series).
   A Yale historian, Prof. Wandycz provides the American
reader, both layman and scholar, with a comprehensive review
of Poland's modern history (especially in the 20th c.),
Polish-American relations (Wilson, FDR), the origins of the
Cold War, and the Cold War itself.

11. Zochowski, Stanislaw. *Brytyjska polityka wobec Polski
1916-1948 /Britain's Policy towards Poland 1916-1948/.*
Brisbane: Maria and Stanislaw Zochowski, 1979. 421p., bibl.
   Based on the author's PhD dissertation at Queensland
University, Australia. A former soldier and diplomat,
Zochowski uses this book as a platform for his "private war"
against Britain's policy towards Poland from World War I to
the beginnings of the Communist rule.

1b. SOCIAL, POLITICAL, AND ECONOMIC HISTORY

12. Bieganski, Witold, ed. *Military Technique, Policy and
Strategy in History.* Warsaw: Ministry of National Defence
Publ. House, 1976. 922p., ill., bibl. Translated from Polish
manuscript.
   This three-part book is a collection of papers dealing,
respectively, with the development of military art and
science throughout centuries, the Poles' participation in the
US War of Independence, and the problems of Poland's policy
and strategy during World War II.

13. Cynk, Jerzy B. *History of the Polish Air Force,
1918-1968.* Reading, England: Osprey Pub., 1972. 307p., ill.
   The author suggests that due to the vast subject the book
should be looked upon as an outline of Polish Air Force (PAF)
history rather than as a source of detailed and fully
comprehensive information. For this reason, technical details
and performance characteristics of Polish aircraft are outside the scope of this study. According to the author, the
book is the first work in world aviation history to cover the
history of the PAF from its inception to the last publication
available to him. The work is organized into six chapters: 1.
"Birth of the PAF"; 2. "The PAF in the fight for Poland's

independence, Nov. 1918-Oct. 1920"; 3. "Years of Peace,
1921-39"; 4. "War over Poland, Sep. 1939"; 5. "Poland's part
in the air war on the side of the Western allies, 1940-45";
6. "The PAF of the Polish People's Republic".

14. Taylor, Jack. *Economic Development of Poland, 1919-1950*.
Ithaca, N.Y.: Cornell University Press, 1952. 222p., bibl.
  A study of the economic history of Poland during the
interwar years, the Nazi-Soviet occupation, and the postwar
development of the planned economy.

2

PRE-WAR PERIOD, 1919–1939

2a. GENERAL ACCOUNTS

15. Coutouvidis, John, and Jaime Reynolds. *Poland, 1939-1947.*
Leicester, UK: Leicester University Press, 1986. 393p.,
plates, ill., maps, bibl. (Politics of Liberation series).
  Based in part on the dissertation of one of the authors,
this study concentrates on Poland's politics, government, and
ruling circles of the pre- and post-war period. For the
period 1939-44, the authors' attention is focused on the
relationship between Churchill's and Sikorski's governments.
The second half gives a good picture of the intensity of the
struggle for power between the parties and individuals
forming the postwar coalition government.

16. Polonsky, Antony. *Politics in Independent Poland
1929-1939: The Crisis of Constitutional Government.* Oxford:
Clarendon Press, 1972. 572p., maps, portraits, bibl.
  This is an account of Polish political life from the end of
the Polish-Soviet war to the defeat of Poland by the Nazi
Germany, set against the social and economic background of
the rebirth of the state. Describes the failure of the
democratic constitution adopted in March 1921 and its
replacement by the semi-autocratic regime of Marshal
Pilsudski and his successors.

17. Watt, Richard M. *Bitter Glory: Poland and Its Fate,
1918-1939.* New York: Simon & Schuster, 1978. 511p., ill.,
portraits, bibl.
  A popular political history of the Polish republic, from
its reconstruction at the end of the First World War to its
partition betwen Nazi Germany and the Soviet Union.

2b. SOCIAL, POLITICAL, AND ECONOMIC HISTORY

18. Gross, Feliks. *The Polish Worker: A Study of Social
Stratum.* Translated by Norbert Guterman. New York: Roy
Publishers, 1945. 274p., bibl.

An analysis of the history and structure of the Polish
labor movement since World War I. Describes the standard of
living of the Polish worker, which was among the lowest in
interwar Europe. A full account of the Nazi treatment of
Polish workers and of the Polish underground struggle is also
added.

19. Kaiser, David E. *Economic Diplomacy and the Origins of
the Second World War: Germany, Britain, France, and East
Europe, 1930- 1939*. Princeton: Princeton University Press,
1980. 346p., bibl.
   The rivalry of the great powers for economic (and hence
political) influence in East Europe in the 1930s. Emphasizes
the key role of Germany's trade policy after 1936 and her
ability to achieve her goals by linking economic objectives
and foreign policy.

20. Roszkowski, Wojciech. *Landowners in Poland, 1918-1939*.
Boulder; New York: East European Monographs; Distributed by
Columbia University Press, 1991. 203p., map, bibl. (East
European Monographs, No. 299).
   Describes the role of large landowners in interwar Poland.
Evaluates their economic, political, and sociocultural
contributions to the development of a new Poland.

21. Wiles, Timothy, ed. *Poland between the Wars, 1918-1939*.
Bloomington, Ind.: Indiana University Polish Studies Center,
1989. 319p., bibl. "A collection of papers and discussions
from the Conference ... held in Bloomington, Indiana,
February 21-23, 1985".
   This book contains twenty-three scholarly essays arranged
to illuminate three broad subjects: Polish interwar political
history (including foreign policy), the country's social
groups, and cultural criticism.

22. Wiskemann, Elizabeth. *Europe of the Dictators, 1919-1945*.
New York: Harper, 1965. 287p.. maps, tables, bibl.
   Primarily a political history of Europe, although including
economic and intellectual aspects. The role of smaller
nations is also discussed. Chapter "The Fall of Poland,
1932-1939" briefly covers the internal history and diplomatic
activities of this period.

2c. INTERNATIONAL SITUATION PRIOR TO THE WAR

23. Batowski, Henryk. *Dyplomacja niemiecka, 1919-1945; zarys
informacyjny /German Diplomacy, 1919-1945, An Outline/*.
Katowice: Slaski Instytut Naukowy, 1971. 103p., bibl.
Summary in English and Russian.
   A short account of the organization of the German Ministry
of Foreign Affairs ("Auswaertige Amt") and its developmental
phases during the period of the Weimar Republic and the
following Third Reich. Discusses the activities of the Berlin
headquarters in the inter-war years, considers ideological
and resulting personnel changes. Main goals, directions, and
methods of the new German diplomacy are shown in relation to
the internal and external policies of the Reich.

24. _____ . *Europa zmierza ku przepasci. /Europe Is
Gravitating to the Precipice/*. Poznan: Wyd. Pozn., 1977.
517p., ill., plates, bibl. Summary in English and Russian.
   Analysis of the events that took place in Europe between
Munich Conference at the end of September 1938 and the German
aggression against Poland 11 months later. These events,
which the author shows in their mutual context, led
consequently to the Second World War.

25. Batowski, Henryk, ed. *Irredenta niemiecka w Europie
srodkowej i poludniowo-wschodniej przed II wojna swiatowa
/German Irredentists in Central and Eastern Europe before the
Second World War/*. Krakow: Panstwowe Wyd. Naukowe, 1971.
281p., maps, bibl. Summary in English, German, and Russian.
   A collection of essays by a team of East European
historians. They discuss the roles and activities of the
German minorities living in Central and South-East European
countries but maintaining particularly close links with the
Reich, and with social and Nazi party organizations.

26. Blanke, Richard. *Orphans of Versailles: The Germans in
Western Poland, 1918-1939*. Lexington, Ky: University Press of
Kentucky, 1993. 316p., bibl.
   The German minority in the territories ceded to Poland
after WW I has been studied mainly as a function of German-
Polish relations, an argument in Germany's revisionist
foreign policy. This book focuses on the minority itself, and
analyzes its plight and dilemma. Poland found this minority a
challenge and regarded Germany's refusal to accept her
postwar frontiers as well as German support of the minority
as threats to her newly restored sovereignty. Blanke
concludes that Germany's political and financial assistance
was the only way the minority could survive. Such growing
dependence made the minority subservient to German policy,
foreclosing any possibility of coming to terms with the
Polish majority.

27. Cienciala, Anna M. *Poland and the Western Powers
1938-1939: A Study in the Interdependence of Eastern and
Western Europe*. Toronto: University of Toronto Press, 1968.
310p., maps, plates. bibl.
   A revaluation and analysis of Poland's role between the
interests of the major western states and her determination
to play a dominant role in Eastern Europe against Germany and
the Soviet Union. The author's main thesis is that Poland
owed her existence to the temporary weakness of her major
neighbors.

28. Karski, Jan. *The Great Powers and Poland, 1919-1945: From
Versailles to Yalta*. Lanham, Maryland: University Press of
America, 1985. 697p., bibl.
   Considers the effects of European diplomacy on the fate of
Poland. Karski criticizes Polish Foreign Minister Jozef Beck,
as well as British, French, and American relations with
Poland but fails to offer any alternatives for the policies
to which he objects. Karski's account is a good companion
volume to R. Debicki and E. Rozek's works. The review in
Choice (Oct. 85) raises one point: "The bibliography of more
than 40 pages in this book reveals how much the existing

literature reflects the importance of interwar Poland and
especially its diplomacy before and during World War II...".

29. Komjathy, Anthony Tihamer, and Rebecca Stockwell. *German
Minorities and the Third Reich: Ethnic Germans in East
Central Europe between the Wars*. New York: Holmes & Meier,
1980. 217p., bibl.
   The German minorities in Poland, Czechoslovakia, Hungary,
Romania and Yugoslavia, their role and activities, and their
relationship with the Nazi Germany.

30. Lukacs, John Adalbert. *Great Powers and Eastern Europe*.
New York: American Book Co., 1953. 878p., maps, bibl.
   This large volume analyzes events in eastern Europe between
1934 (when Soviet Russia decided to enter the League of
Nations) and 1945. Although the book deals with the Great
Powers, it focuses primarily on the fate of smaller central
and eastern European countries, from Finland, the Baltic
states, through Poland and Czechoslovakia, to the Danubian
and Balkan states in the south. Their activities are shown in
relation to the policies of the giants, the Soviet Russia in
particular.

31. Lumans, Valdis O. *Himmler's Auxiliaries: The Volksdeutsche Mittelstelle and the German National Minorities of
Europe, 1933-1945*. Chapel Hill: University of North Carolina
Press, 1993. 335p., maps, bibl.
   This study focuses on the relations of the ethnic Germans
(known as *Volksdeutsche*) in particular European countries
(Baltic, Central, Southeast, West, and the Soviet Union) with
the Third Reich. These relations are discussed within the
context of Hitler's foreign policy, as well as of the ideas,
goals and plans of Heinrich Himmler, the Reichsfuehrer SS,
directly responsible for coordinating the minorities'
activities during the period of 1933-45. Among the issues
addressed are individual roles of the Volksdeutsche groups in
their countries and the process of nazification. Recommended
as a good sequel to the Komjathy volume.

32. Namier, Lewis Bernstein. *Diplomatic Prelude 1938-1939*.
London: Macmillan, 1948. 503p., bibl.
   An important study of the diplomatic situation in East-
Central Europe during 1938-1939. Contains series of Polish
and Czech documents for September-October 1938. Two chapters
are of special concern. Chapter 2, "From Munich to Prague--
September 29th, 1938, to March 15th, 1939", brings a vivid
examination of the consequences of Munich Agreement and the
value of Western guarantees to the Rump Czechoslovakia. In
chapter 8 the author analyzes the political situation in
Berlin in the months prior to the invasion of Poland.

33. _____. *Europe in Decay: A Study in Disintegration
1936-1940*. London: Macmillan, 1950. 329p., bibl.
   A study of European diplomacy during 1936-1940. This is a
critical analysis of documents, memoirs, and monographs that
appeared after the publication of Namier's *Diplomatic
Prelude*.

34. _____ . *In the Nazi Era*. New York: St. Martin's Press,
1952. 203p., bibl.
   This is the last of Namier's books on the subject of East-
Central Europe, and a continuation of his previous
publications (see the titles above).

35. Prochazka, Theodore. *The Second Republic: The Disintegration of Post-Munich Czecholovakia, October 1938-March 1939*.
Boulder, New York: Distributed by Columbia University Press,
1981. 231p., maps, bibl. Based on the author's PhD disserta-
tion at the University of Paris, 1954, under the title "La
Tchecoslovaquie de Munich a Mars 1939".
   This study deals with the period in Czech history from the
Munich Agreement of 1938 to the establishment of a German
protectorate over Bohemia and Moravia in March 1939. Divided
into five chapters, which cover the implementation of the
Munich Four Powers' *Diktat* and the negotiations carried on by
Prague with Berlin, Bratislava, Budapest, and Warsaw.

36. Radice, Lisanne. *Prelude to Appeasement: East Central
European Diplomacy in the Early 1930's*. Boulder & New York:
East European Quarterly; distributed by Columbia University
Press, 1981. 218p., bibl. (East European Monographs, no. 80).
   A history of the unsuccessful negotiations, from 1933 to
March 1936, concerning a multinational Eastern Locarno Pact.
The book devotes special attention to Poland, which the
author terms here as the 'lynchpin' of the eastern pact
security system. Radice provides new information concerning
British and Polish diplomacy based on their foreign
ministries' records and some private papers. A very detailed
study.

37. Toynbee, Arnold Joseph, and Veronica Toynbee. *The Eve of
War, 1939*. London: Oxford University Press, 1958. 744p.,
ill., portraits, maps, bibl.
   A careful analysis of British and German documents related
to their foreign policy for a few months between Hitler's
occupation of Czechoslovakia and Poland.

38. U.S. Government. Department of State. *Foreign Relations
of the United States. Diplomatic Papers, 1938-1939*.
Washington, D.C.: U.S. Printing Office, 1955-1956.
   Large collection of American diplomatic papers. The volumes
provide a general picture of the international situation
during the critical period 1938-39. For Poland and other
European countries consult index in each volume.

39. Wheeler-Bennett, John W. *Munich: Prologue to Tragedy*.
London: Macmillan, 1966. 508p., maps, ill., bibl.
   Drawn mainly from a variety of white, blue, and yellow
books published during WW II. Chapter 9 (Pt 2) provides a
survey of Polish foreign policy in the interwar period.

40. Wiskemann, Elizabeth. *Europe of the Dictators, 1919-1945*.
New York: Harper, 1965. 287p.. maps, tables, bibl.
   Primarily a political history of Europe, although including
economic and intellectual aspects. The role of smaller
nations is also discussed. Chapter "The Fall of Poland,
1932-1939" briefly covers the internal history and diplomatic

activities of this period.

2d. FOREIGN RELATIONS (including relations with Danzig)

41. Beck, Jozef. *Final Report*. New York: Robert Speller and
Sons, 1957. 278p., ill., portraits.
   An historical account of Polish foreign policy through the
author's activities from 1926 to 1939. Last section provides,
in effect, fragments of a study relating to twenty years of
international politics. Many portraits of the author during
his life.

42. Biddle, Anthony Joseph Drexel. *Poland and the Coming of
the Second World War: The Diplomatic Papers of A.J. Drexel
Biddle, Jr., United States Ambassador to Poland, 1937-1939*,
ed. with an introd. by Philip V. Cannistraro. Columbus: Ohio
State University, 1976. 358p., ill.
   Biddle was appointed ambassador to Poland in mid-1937.
After the German invasion in Sept. 1939, he accompanied the
Polish government into exile, remaining accredited to it
until 1944. This selection of his reports to Roosevelt covers
the Warsaw tenure. The volume affords some good insights into
complex aspects of Polish history and rehabilitates Polish
pre-war diplomacy "fared poorly in standard studies". It also
contributes to understanding the European crisis and U.S.
diplomacy on the eve of the Second World War.

43. Blanke, Richard. *Orphans of Versailles: The Germans in
Western Poland, 1918-1939*. Lexington, Ky: University Press of
Kentucky, 1993. 316p., bibl.
   The German minority in the territories ceded to Poland
after WW I has been studied mainly as a function of German-
Polish relations, an argument in Germany's revisionist
foreign policy. This book focuses on the minority itself, and
analyzes its plight and dilemma. Poland found this minority a
challenge and regarded Germany's refusal to accept her
postwar frontiers as well as German support of the minority
as threats to her newly restored sovereignty. Blanke
concludes that Germany's political and financial assistance
was the only way the minority could survive. Such growing
dependence made the minority subservient to German policy,
foreclosing any possibility of coming to terms with the
Polish majority.

44. Budurowycz, Bohdan Basil. *Polish-Soviet Relations,
1932-1939*. New York: Columbia University Press, 1963. 229p.,
bibl. (East Central European Studies).
   An assessment of the relationship between Poland and the
USSR and of Poland's policy of attempting to play off Germany
against the USSR and to maintain a balance between the two.

45. Debicki, Roman. *Foreign Policy of Poland, 1919-1939: From
the Rebirth of the Polish Republic to World War II*. New York:
Praeger, 1962. 192p., bibl.
   Although entitled *Foreign Policy of Poland...*, Prof.
Debicki's book is actually an excellent survey of European
diplomacy in the interwar period. As a member for many years
of the Polish diplomatic service, Debicki adds firsthand

experience to the careful analysis of printed and private
sources available to him to appraise the shaping of Polish
foreign policy. Describes Poland's quest for stability and
security amid the provocations and expansionist policies of
Germany and the Soviet Union. Analyzes Poland's search for a
system of alliances in the interwar period. Explains the
background and origins of World War II from Warsaw's point of
view.

46. Henderson, H. W. *An Outline of Polish-Soviet Relations*.
Glasgow: Polish Information Center, 1946. 36p., ill., maps.
   Brief survey of Russo-Polish relations with emphasis on the
period from 1918 onwards. Attempts to justify Polish claims
to territories taken from Poland by Russia in 1939.

47. Kimmich, Christoph M. *The Free City: Danzig and German
Foreign Policy, 1919-1934*. New Haven: Yale University Press,
1968. 196p., map, bibl.
   A concise, thorough study of relations between Danzig,
Germany and Poland. Traces the role of Danzig in German
foreign policy and that of German domination of the internal
affairs of Danzig from its establishing as the Free City to
the signing of the German-Polish Declaration of Non-
Aggression in January 1934. Although based mainly on German
and western sources, archival and published (no Polish items
listed), the book is a useful addition to studies of the
diplomatic problems of the interwar years.

48. Komjathy, Anthony Tihamer, and Rebecca Stockwell. *German
Minorities and the Third Reich: Ethnic Germans in East
Central Europe between the Wars*. New York: Holmes & Meier,
1980. 217p., bibl.
   The German minorities in Poland, Czechoslovakia, Hungary,
Romania and Yugoslavia, their role and activities, and their
relationship with the Nazi Germany.

49. Konovalov, Serge, ed. *Russo-Polish Relations: An
Historical Survey*. Princeton: Princeton University Press,
1945. 110p., maps, bibl.
   The principal purpose of the survey is to report Polish-
Russian conflicts over the area east of the Curzon line and
to show the nationality composition of the 11,000,000 people
living there in 1931. Despite its somewhat pro-Russian bias,
this volume throws helpful light on a knotty problem.

50. Korbel, Josef. *Poland between East and West: Soviet and
German Diplomacy toward Poland, 1919-1933*. Princeton, NJ:
Princeton University Press, 1963. 320p., bibl.
   This study of diplomacy covers the period between the
Russo-Polish War of 1920 and the Declaration of Non-
Aggression between Poland and Germany in January 1934. A
Czech historian has made a thorough use of Polish, Russian
and German primary language sources to depict in this
excellent account political atmospheres in Berlin and Moscow.
Whatever the opportunities, the goal of that diplomacy, as
always in the past, was only one: to forge a front against
Poland and cause, in consequence, her subsequent partition.
The reader will find in this book a multitude of exciting
accounts concerning the main political figures of the time,

such, for instance, as an episode of secret talks between
Marshal Pilsudski's emissaries and Lenin at Mikaszewice. Dr.
Korbel's book is a good companion volume to Bohdan
Budurowycz's *Polish-Soviet Relations* ..., which should go
second.

51. Korczynski, Alexander, and Tadeusz Swietochowski, eds.
Poland between Germany and Russia: The Theory of Two Enemies.
New York: Pilsudski Institute of America, 1975. 72p.
    Collection of papers delivered at Columbia University in
1974 on the apparent dilemma which Poland faced during the
fateful thirteen years prior to the outbreak of World War II.

52. Kulski, Wladyslaw W. *Germany and Poland: From War to
Peaceful Relations*. Syracuse: Syracuse University Press,
1976. 336p., bibl.
    An analysis of both the Polish and German points of view
regarding their mutual relations during the pre- and post-war
periods. It also covers West German-Polish relations through
the 1970s. The author places these relations in the broader
context of Europe's security issues, East-West detente, and
German reunification.

53. Lipski, Jozef. *Diplomat in Berlin, 1933-1939: Papers and
Memoirs of Jozef Lipski, Ambassador of Poland*. Ed. by Waclaw
Jedrzejewicz. New York: Columbia University Press, 1968.
679p., bibl.
    This volume contains documents from the files of Jozef
Lipski, the Polish ambassador in Berlin during the years 1933
through 1939. Arranged chronologically, they cover
conversations with Hitler, Goering, Neurath, and Ribbentrop.
Also included are documents on the negotiaion of the
Polish-German Non-Aggression Pact, the quarrel over Danzig,
the Anschluss, the Czechoslovak crisis, and the outbreak of
war. These materials provide an excellent view of the
Polish-German relations. The book is the sad story of a
policy that failed--the policy of reconciliation or even
partnership between the two countries.

54. Lukasiewicz, Juliusz. *Diplomat in Paris, 1936-1939:
Papers and Memoirs of Juliusz Lukasiewicz, Ambassador of
Poland*. New York: Columbia University Press, 1970. 408p.,
ill., portraits, bibl.
    The role played by the Polish Ambassador in Paris in a
constantly worsening international situation. The major
themes discussed are the frustrations of dealing with naive
and uninformed allies, who refused to recognize the threat of
the dictators, along with the necessity of continually
requiring assurances of support from a reluctant French ally.
The book is a companion volume to a similar collection of
Lipski's *Diplomat in Berlin*.

55. Mackiewicz, Stanislaw. *Colonel Beck and His Policy*.
London: Eyre and Spottiswood, Ltd., 1951. 139p.
    Presents a complete picture of the foreign policy of Poland
as handled by Colonel Jozef Beck from his accession as
Vice-Minister for Foreign Affairs in November 1932 until the
invasion of Poland in September 1939. It is an analysis of
the policy, not the man. Not documented.

56. Mason, John Brown. *The Danzig Dilemma: A Study in Peacemaking by Compromise*. Stanford: Stanford University Press, 1946. 377p., facs, tabl., bibl.
   A detailed, documented study of the part the City of Danzig had played in international affairs for over a thousand years. Focuses on the political and economic problems of Danzig presented at the Paris Peace Conference (1918) and on the administrative problems which arose while Danzig was under the protection of the League of Nations. The author concludes by pointing out to possible compromises and solutions in future peacemaking attempts.

57. Pease, Neal. *Poland, the United States, and the Stabilization of Europe, 1919-1933*. New York: Oxford University Press, 1986. 238p., bibl.
   This is a thoughtful analysis of the mutual relations of the United States and Poland from the perspective of American stabilization policy in interwar Europe. Pease demonstrates that the stabilization policy in Poland convinced the United States there was the need to solve the problems of Central and East Europe as a precondition of a peaceful European continent. In this light, Pease points out, a stabilization of economic and political conditions in Poland became one of the more important goals of the U.S. financial diplomacy in the interwar period. This is a valuable account of the subject because the author seeks to view Polish-American relations in the larger European context.

58. Poland. Ministerstwo Spraw Zagranicznych. *Official Documents Concerning Polish-German and Polish-Soviet Relations, 1933-1939*. London, New York: Hutchinson, Roy, 1940. 222p. On cover: "The Polish White Book".
   Known as the *Polish White Book*, this is a collection of documents dealing mostly with diplomatic relations between Poland, Germany, and the Soviet Russia in the years 1933-39. Published by the Polish Government-in-Exile.

59. Roberts, Henry L. *"The Diplomacy of Colonel Beck"*. *The Diplomats 1919-1939*. Edited by Gordon A. Craig and Felix Gilbert. Princeton: Princeton University Press, 1953. 700p., portraits, bibl.
   This chapter by Roberts is a study of Colonel Jozef Beck, the Polish Minister for Foreign Affairs 1932-1939. An interesting evaluation of the man and his policy.

60. Shotwell, James T., and Max M. Laserson. *Poland and Russia, 1919-1945*. New York: Carnegie Endowment for International Peace, 1945. 114p., maps, bibl.
   A scholarly and impartial investigation of the history of the complicated dealings between the two countries during the period from the restoration of Poland after World War I to 1945. Texts of important documents are included. The book may help understand the Polish problem.

61. Super, Margaret L. *Poland and Russia: The Last Quarter Century*. New York: Sheed and Ward, 1945. 251p., maps, bibl.
   History of Polish-Soviet relations between 1918 and 1943. Based upon innumerable conversations, letters, and a mass of

documentary material. The author lived in Poland with her
husband from 1922 to 1939.

62. Umiastowski, Roman. *Russia and the Polish Republic,
1918-1941*. London: "Aquafondata", 1945. 319p., ill., maps,
bibl.
    An account of the centuries-old dispute between the
Russians and the Poles. Focus on events from 1939 to 1941.

63. Von Riekhoff, Harald. *German-Polish Relations, 1918-1933*.
Baltimore: John Hopkins Press, 1971. 421p., bibl.
    In this lengthy analysis of the diplomatic relations
between the nascent Polish and German republics, the author
discusses the clash of German revisionism in Eastern Europe
with the Polish dedication to the maintenance of the status
quo in the interwar years. Setting the dispute in its
international context, the book objectively and
comprehensively handles a centuries-old, complex and
significant problem and shows the interplay of the European
diplomatic forces on the German-Polish disagreements. The
author draws heavily upon German and Polish documentary
materials.

64. Wandycz, Piotr Stefan. *The Twilight of French Eastern
Alliances, 1926-1936: French-Czechoslovak-Polish Relations
from Locarno to the Remilitarization of the Rhineland*.
Princeton, N.J.: Princeton University Press, 1988. 537p.,
bibl.
    A monumental, detailed scholarly study of the evolving
political, economic, and military relations between France,
Poland, and Czechoslovakia in the decade following the
Locarno Pacts. Wandycz explores the forces that led to the
disintegration of the French eastern alliances. Essential to
an understanding of the larger European issues of the
interwar period.

65. Weinberg, Gerhard L. *The Foreign Policy of Hitler's
Germany: Diplomatic Revolution in Europe, 1933-36*. Chicago:
University of Chicago Press, 1970. 397p., bibl.
    A masterly analysis of the foreign policy of Hitler
Germany. Professor Weinberg has fully utilized the published
and manuscript sources which were available to him. This book
is valuable for the country-by-country survey of Hitler's
foreign policy. Aspects of German-Polish relations have been
referred to several times, but got a closer look in chapter
3, "Eastern Europe", in which Weinberg discusses German
policy toward Poland, the Soviet Union, Lithuania and the
Ukraine in 1933. The discussion of Polish-German relations
covers territorial issues (Silesia, Danzig), German minority,
and the January 1934 Non-Aggression Pact.

66. Weyers, J. *Poland and Russia*. London: Barnard and
Westwood, Ltd., 1945. 64p., ill., maps.
    Outline of Polish-Russian relations, 1921-1942, prior to
break in relations between Polish government-in-exile and the
U.S.S.R. Takes anti-Soviet viewpoint.

67. Winid, Boguslaw W. *W cieniu Kapitolu: dyplomacja polska wobec Stanow Zjednoczonych Ameryki, 1919-1939* /In the Shadow of Capitol Hill: Polish Diplomacy and the United States of America, 1919-1939/. Warszawa: Pomost, 1991. 268p., bibl. Summary in English.

A comprehensive review of Polish-American relations during interwar from Poland's perspective. Focuses on aims and problems of the young diplomacy. Concludes that in spite of numerous internal and external difficulties and obstacles, the Polish diplomacy of this period was able to achieve, to a certain extent, the main goal: to convince Americans that the reborn Polish state "was a permanent and necessary element of the international order." The book is a good sequel to Pease's study.

68. Wojciechowski, Marian. *Stosunki polsko-niemieckie 1933-1938* / Polish-German Relations, 1933-1938/. Poznan: Instytut Zachodni, 1980. 558p., bibl. Summary in English, German and Russian.

An in-depth study of Polish-German relations between the Non-Aggression Pact 1934 and Munich 1938. A special emphasis is placed on the close links between the internal situations and foreign policies of both countries.

3

WAR ORIGINS AND OUTBREAK

3a. GENERAL ACCOUNTS

69. Aster, Sidney. *The Making of the Second World War*. New
York: Simon & Schuster, 1973. 645p., ill., bibl.
    Aster, a British historian, has consulted the published and
unpublished State papers of Europe, including the British
Parliament, the USSR, and North America, for the purpose of
this work. The readers learn that Hitler's occupation of
Czechoslovakia finally convinced the Allies of his intent.
They learn why Poland was not better supported in her death
struggle with the enemy, and why the Allies and the Nazis
both kept talking to Soviet Russia. "It is a record of
astonishing ineptitude on the part of the British Cabinet and
some of its diplomats during the period between March 15,
1939 and Sept. 3, when Britain declared war." (*NYT Bk R*. Mr
24 '74 p 24).

70. Ball, Adrian. *The Last Day of the Old World: 3rd
September, 1939*. Garden City, N.Y.: Doubleday, 1963. 291p.,
ill., bibl.
    This study focuses on the day when World War II was
declared. The book is divided into four parts: midnight to 6
a.m.; 6 a.m. to noon; noon to 6 p.m.; 6 p.m. to midnight, all
concerned with the fateful day of September 3, 1939. The
author constructs a vivid examination of reactions and
thoughts of the leaders of Britain, France, Italy, Germany
and Poland, and the decisions that Britain and France at last
made to go to the aid of invaded Poland.

71. Carr, William. *Poland to Pearl Harbor, the Making of the
Second World War*. London: E. Arnold, 1985. 183p., maps, bibl.
    Examines the causes of World War II from a global
perspective. Sets out to question a number of generally held
opinions about the political and strategic issues underlying
the early years of the war. Carr treats only Germany, Japan,
and the United States as principals in the making of the war.
The Soviet Union and Great Britain play only a secondary
role. The *Times Lit Suppl's* (Aug 9, 1985) reviewer sums up:

"This is not a very flattering appreciation of Britain's
role, but it may be nearer the truth than the traditional
Anglocentric analysis of 1941 that has been with us since
Churchill wrote his war memoirs".

72. Cieplewicz, Mieczyslaw. *Wojna obronna Polski, 1939
/Poland's Defensive War of 1939/*. Warszawa: Military
Historical Institute, 1979. 949p., plates, ill., maps, bibl.
Summary and table of contents in English and Russian.
    Poland's defensive war of 1939 and the subsequent collapse
of the state was a great tragedy for the Polish people. How
did it happen that a state which had existed for less than 21
years again fell into a five-year cruel bondage? The work is
an attempt at answering this question. It consists of two
parts. The first deals with the origins of the war, the
second presents its course.

73. Debicki, Roman. *Foreign Policy of Poland, 1919-1939: From
the Rebirth of the Polish Republic to World War II*. New York:
Praeger, 1962. 192p., bibl.
    Although entitled *Foreign Policy of Poland...*, Prof.
Debicki's book is actually an excellent survey of European
diplomacy in the interwar period. As a member for many years
of the Polish diplomatic service, Debicki adds firsthand
experience to the careful analysis of printed and private
sources available to him to appraise the shaping of Polish
foreign policy. Describes Poland's quest for stability and
security amid the provocations and expansionist policies of
Germany and the Soviet Union. Analyzes Poland's search for a
system of alliances in the interwar period. Explains the
background and origins of World War II from Warsaw's point of
view.

74. Haines, Charles Grove, and Ross John Swartz Hoffman.
*Origins and Background of the Second World War. 2nd ed.,
revised and enlarged*. New York: Oxford University Press,
1947. 729p., maps, bibl.
    A summary of the political conditions and events which led
up to the outbreak of the Second World War. The time covered
is from about 1900 to the close ot 1941. The effects of
Fascist, Nazi, and Communist ideologies and their
repercussions on international affairs are shown. The
Ethiopian, Spanish, Austrian, Czechoslovak, and Polish crises
are all traced and put in the perspective of growing European
complications.

75. Kaiser, David E. *Economic Diplomacy and the Origins of
the Second World War: Germany, Britain, France, and East
Europe, 1930- 1939*. Princeton: Princeton University Press,
1980. 346p., bibl.
    The rivalry of the great powers for economic (and hence
political) influence in East Europe in the 1930s. Emphasizes
the key role of Germany's trade policy after 1936 and her
ability to achieve her goals by linking economic objectives
and foreign policy.

76. Lukacs, John Adalbert. *The Last European War, September
1939-December 1941*. New York: Anchor Press, 1976. 562p.,
bibl.

The first section of this book is a summary of the events
leading to Hitler's invasion of Poland, and the Franco-
British declaration of war, and of the course of that war in
Europe until the Japanese attack on Pearl Harbor. The second
section is a study of Europeans' social, political,
intellectual and artistic life in that era.

77. Machray, Robert. *East Prussia: Menace to Poland and
Peace*. London: George Allen & Unwin Ltd., 1944. 112p., ill.,
maps, bibl., appendices.
    The book has been written for the British and American
public who have little or no knowledge about the province. It
shows how many of the deep troubles that darkened Europe and
the world prior to and during the wartime found a most
significant share of their origin in Germany's hold on that
tract of land on the Southern Baltic. It was Germany's
bastion thrust towards the East, but will lose, Mr. Machray
believes, that character if handed to Poland. The author
demonstrates the economic failure of German exploitation of
East Prussia and explains why greatly improved results are to
be expected if it is peopled by Poles. The book also deals
with the population problems inevitably involved in such a
policy.

78. Matuszewski, Ignacy. *Great Britain's Obligations towards
Poland and Some Facts about the Curzon Line*. New York:
National Committee of Americans of Polish Descent, 1947.
85p., ill., maps.
    Written with fairness, this book presents the reciprocal
obligations of Great Britain and Poland as based upon the
Agreement of Mutual Assistance of August 25, 1939.

79. Newman, Simon. *March 1939: The British Guarantee to
Poland: A Study in the Continuity of British Foreign Policy*.
Oxford: Clarendon Press, 1976. 253p., bibl.
    A scholarly complementary study to the still growing
literature on the origins of World War Two. Also useful as a
contribution to the on-going appraisal of British policy
during the last period before the outbreak when "the
deliberations and decisions of Whitehall swayed the destinies
of entire continents".

80. Overy, Richard J., and Andrew Wheatcroft. *The Road to
War*. London: Macmillan, 1989. 364p. plates, ill, maps, bibl.
    "The question why the great powers found themselves at war
with Hitler has been asked many times and the answers are
rather simple: Hitler had to be stopped; the weak and
defenseless western democracies finally rediscovered their
courage; Poland had to be defended. But recent historical
research has shown that all the issues are much more complex
than these simple answers would suggest. It was France and
Britain, not Germany, who expected war in 1939. Hitler had
assumed that his takeover of Poland would be unopposed. *The
Road to War* is a controversial and challenging study trying
to show how the world's states entered the conflict." (From
the publisher's review).

81. Saunders, Alan. *The Invasion of Poland.* New York: F.
Watts, 1984. 104p., ill., bibl.
Traces the history of Poland, emphasizing the events
leading to September 1939, the invasion of Poland by the
armies of Germany and Russia.

82. Smith, Gene. *The Dark Summer: An Intimate History of the
Events that Led to World War II.* New York: Macmillan, 1987.
314p., ill., photos, bibl.
England, Germany, Russia, their leaders, and some lesser-
known figures of the European political scene are the focus.
Against this background Smith retraces the factors that led
to World War II, from the death of Czechoslovakia to the
Russo-German pact to the intimidation, then the destruction
of Poland.

83. Strzetelski, Stanislaw. *Where the Storm Broke.* New York:
Roy Slavonic Publications, 1943. 257p.
An account of international events leading to World War II
as they affected Poland, of war itself and life in the
country under the Nazi occupation. A journalist, Strzelecki
writes from personal knowledge, diaries, letters, and
official documents. Not always interesting or convincing, the
book may be considered useful as one of early accounts of the
subject and a valuable introduction to the Polish view of the
interwar period, differing notably from views most Americans
and Britons held on these points.

84. Watt, Donald Cameron. *How War Came: The Immediate Origins
of the Second World War, 1938-1939.* London: Heinemann, 1989.
736p., plates, ill., maps, portraits, bibl.
This is a study of European diplomacy during the eleven
months between the 1938 Munich conference and Hitler's
invasion of Poland.

85. Weinberg, Gerhard L. *The Foreign Policy of Hitler's
Germany: Starting World War II, 1937-1939.* Chicago:
University of Chicago Press, 1980. 728p., map, bibl.
This volume concludes the author's analysis of German
foreign policy. He attempts to demonstrate in this book that
from 1937 to 1939 Hitler dominated German foreign relations,
which had only one direction: domination of Europe through
intimidation and, if necessary, a general European war.
According to this interpretation, Hitler planned to expand
Germany (the Lebensraum strategy) by conquering Poland, other
East European countries, and the Soviet Union, moving step by
step to eliminate all resistance, especially from the Western
powers.

86. Wiskemann, Elizabeth. *Undeclared War.* 2nd ed. London:
Macmillan, 1967. 332p., bibl.
This second edition is an attempt to provide an accurate
review of Germany's prewar preparations. Published in the
U.S. 1940 under the title *Prologue to War*, it was originally
written in the summer of 1939 just before Hitler's attack on
Poland. It is a picture of a Europe overawed by the German
titan, and the author shows how easy it was for the Germans
after their Munich triumph to penetrate into eastern Europe.

3b. DANZIG AND SILESIA

87. Henderson, Neville. *Failure of a Mission: Berlin, 1937-1939*. New York: G. P. Putnam's Sons, 1940. 334p.
British ambassador, 1937-1939, determined to promote Anglo-German understanding. Of concern to us are the fragments on the Anschluss, Munich conference, and the crisis over Danzig.

88. Leonhardt, Hans Leo. *Nazi Conquest of Danzig*. Chicago: University of Chicago Press, 1948. 363p., maps, bibl.
A study of the process of Danzig's Nazification from 1930 to 1939. Based on extensive documentation and the author's personal participation as a member of Danzig's opposition party.

89. Levine, Herbert S. *Hitler's Free City: A History of the Nazi Party in Danzig, 1935-1939*. Chicago: University of Chicago Press, 1973. 223p., bibl.
This scholarly work relates with impartiality the progress of the Nazi movement in pre-World War II Danzig. The author points out that the struggle for power in Danzig was possible because of the unique position of Danzig as a free city under the protection of the League of Nations, the status that permitted free elections and political opposition to continue well after the Nazi takeover in Germany.

90. Popiolek, Kazimierz. *Silesia in German Eyes, 1939-1945*. Katowice: Wyd. Slask, 1964. 238p., maps, bibl.
Seeks to explain the germanization of the Slask (Silesia) region prior to and during the German occupation of Poland between 1939 and 1945, and the Polish reaction to these measures.

91. Wiskemann, Elizabeth. *Germany's Eastern Neighbours: Problems Relating to the Oder-Neisse and the Czech Frontier Regions*. London: Oxford University Press, 1956. 309p., maps, bibl. "Issued under the auspices of the Royal Institute of International Affairs."
A detailed, objective discussion of developments in territories of German-Polish and German-Czech controversy in the years since Hitler's rise to power. Wiskemann analyzes the awkward, complex problems of Upper and Lower Silesia, the old "Danzig Corridor", Poznan (Posen), and the rest. Particular emphasis is given to the postwar decade, witnessing the territorial changes, expulsion of the Germans, and the new industrial activities in these lands.

3c. HITLER-STALIN PACT, 1939

92. Grunberg, Karol, and Jerzy Serczyk. *Czwarty rozbior Polski: z dziejow stosunkow radziecko-niemieckich w okresie miedzywojennym /The Fourth Partition of Poland: An Historical Survey of Soviet-German Relations between the Wars/*. Warszawa: Inst. Wydawniczy Zwiazkow Zawodowych, 1990. 325p., ill., bibl. Summary in English, German, and Russian.
The term Fourth Partition of Poland commonly refers to the division of the Polish State in September 1939 between the Third Reich and the Soviet Union. The book surveys the

development of the German-Soviet relations in the interwar
period beginning with 1918, and then comes to the detailed
discussion of the circumstances leading to the Pact (known
also as Nazi-Soviet Non-Aggression Pact, Ribbentrop-Molotov
Pact, or Hitler-Stalin Pact), the course of the negotiations,
the terms of the two Treaties (August 23 and September 28,
1939), and finally the consequences of the Pact for Poland:
its partition.

93. Kolasky, John. *Partners in Tyranny: The Nazi-Soviet
Nonaggression Pact, August 23, 1939*. Toronto: The Mackenzie
Institute, 1990. 158p., plates, ill., bibl.
    Outlines the basis of the Pact, the events leading up to
its formulation, and its terms, consequences, and legacy. The
book traces German-Russian military cooperation back to 1921.
Based on published sources.

94. Read, Anthony, and David Fisher. *The Deadly Embrace:
Hitler, Stalin, and the Nazi-Soviet Pact, 1939-1941*. London:
Michael Joseph, 1988. 687p., plates, ill., maps, portraits,
bibl.
    The authors draw from published sources, as well as
archival materials and interviews for their detailed and most
interesting account of events that led to the pact, the
negotiations, the treaty's consequences for Poland and the
Baltic states. On occasion, the authors note the Soviets'
efforts to pin the massacre of thousands of Polish officers
in the Katyn Forest on the Nazis, but fail to point out that
the evidence of Soviet responsibility is overwhelming.
Nonetheless, this is an important contribution to the history
of the Nazi-Soviet Pact. A good companion volume to the work
by GK Roberts.

95. Roberts, Geoffrey K. *The Unholy Alliance: Stalin's Pact
with Hitler*. Bloomington: Indiana University Press, 1990.
296p., bibl.
    This amply documented study by a British scholar "aims to
explain why Soviet Russia concluded a non-aggression treaty
with Nazi Germany in 1939, to describe the circumstances in
which that decision was taken, and to analyze the
consequences of that action for Soviet foreign policy in the
period before 22 June 1941" (From Introduction). Roberts
makes two fundamental points: the signing of the pact did not
eliminate "hesitancy and ambiguity" from Soviet policy, and
no specific agreement to partition Poland was at first
involved. Like Read and Fisher's book, this is an important
one and deserves to be read by all those who are concerned
with the histories of Stalinism and interwar diplomacy.

4
MILITARY ASPECTS OF
THE WAR

4a. POLAND IN THE SECOND WORLD WAR (general accounts)

96. Cieplewicz, Mieczyslaw. *Wojna obronna Polski, 1939
/Poland's Defensive War of 1939/*. Warszawa: Military
Historical Institute, 1979. 949p., plates, ill., maps, bibl.
Summary and table of contents in English and Russian.
   Poland's defensive war of 1939 and the subsequent collapse
of the state was a great tragedy for the Polish people. How
did it happen that a state which had existed for less than 21
years again fell into a five-year cruel bondage? The work is
an attempt at answering this question. It consists of two
parts. The first deals with the origins of the war, the
second presents its course.

97. Davies, Norman. *Heart of Europe: A Short History of
Poland*. Oxford: Oxford University Press, 1986. 511p., ill.,
bibl.
   The British historian, author of several titles on Polish
history here in chapter 2, "The Legacy of Defeat", gives an
excellent survey of Poland's wartime experience from 1939
through 1947.

98. Garlinski, Jozef. *Poland in the Second World War*. New
York: Hippocrene Books, 1985. 508p., plates, maps, portraits,
bibl.
   The author of numerous popular accounts on various aspects
of the war, Garlinski in this book has skillfully compressed
a mass of information based on western, eastern, and even
Vatican sources to present a one-volume documentary history
of Poland's involvement in World War II. He seeks to treat
"Polish affairs in the context of larger global political and
military concerns." Garlinski also discusses the *Enigma*.

99. Halecki, Oskar. *A History of Poland*. New York: D. McKay
Co., 1976. 366p., plates, maps.
   In two chapters, "Destruction" and "Ten Years of Trial", a
distinguished Polish historian discusses in chronological
order the main aspects of the war: causes, course, military

and diplomatic concerns, and the war's consequences for
Poland.

100. Marszalek, Rafal. *Polska wojna w obcym filmie /The
Polish War in Foreign Motion Pictures/*. Wroclaw: Ossolineum.
Polish Academy of Science Institute of Art, 1978. 170p.,
bibl. Summary in English.
  A review of foreign motion pictures produced in the years
1939-1967 and dealing with wartime Poland. Features unknown
materials and documents.

101. New York Public Library. *Poland in Photographs,
1939-1944*. New York: New York Public Library, 1946. 5 vols.,
ill.
  Mounted and bound in 5 volumes by the New York Public
Library, this most unique massive compilation of photographs
and text gives a comprehensive picture of various aspects of
the nations's life before and during the war. Topics covered
in the particular volumes are: 1. Poland, pre-war 1939; 2.
Poland, German occupation, 1939; 3. Polish children all over
the world. Jews in Poland, 1942-1944; 4. Armed forces of the
Polish government in London, 1942-1944; 5. Polish government
in London. Polish Underground, 1942-1944.

102. Piekalkiewicz, Janusz. *The Cavalry of World War II*.
London: Orbis, 1979. 256p., ill., portraits, bibl.
Translation of *Pferd und Reiter im II Weltkrieg*.
  As the title suggests, the book is about the war on
horseback and includes reports of the military operations by
the mounted units of the nations involved. Many photographs
give a clear idea of the war on horseback.

103. Woods, William. *Poland: Eagle in the East: A Survey of
Modern Times*. New York: Hill & Wang, 1968. 272p., plates,
bibl.
  A panorama of postwar Poland. The book opens with a
discussion of World War II in Poland, the underground, the
Warsaw Ghetto uprising, the death camps, the Battle of
Warsaw, and moves on to the postwar recovery in industry and
farming, the resurgence of the arts and literature, the
postwar political scene, the Communist Party, the Catholic
Church, and Polish attitudes toward Russia and Germany. The
author's "account of the relations between Poles and Jews
before, during, and after the occupation makes a great effort
to be fair in a field where others take leave of their
senses." (Neal Ascherson, *NY Rev of Books*, 12:27 May 8, '69).

104. Wrzos-Glinka, Stanislaw. *We Have Not Forgotten,
1939-1945*. Warsaw: League of Fighters for Freedom and
Democracy, 1959. 266p.
  A mostly-illustrated historical overview of occupation and
war in Poland, with numerous photographs of atrocities.
Supported by statistics on executions and military losses in
all battles in which Polish soldiers fought.

105. Zaloga, Steve, and Victor Madej. *The Polish Campaign
1939*. New York: Hippocrene Books, 1985. 195p., ill., maps,
bibl.
  The aim of this book is to examine the September 1939

campaign from the perspective of the Polish Army. The authors
(well-known specialists on World War II) hope that their
"more detailed appraisal of Polish operational doctrine, the
army organization and conduct in the September fighting will
refocus attention of western historians on these subjects and
make them aware of the wealth of available material" still
awaiting its exploration, particularly in Polish archives.
Richly illustrated.

4b. CAMPAIGNS AND BATTLES

4b1. General Accounts

106. Dziewanowski, M. K. *War at Any Price: World War II in
Europe, 1939-1945*. Englewood Cliffs, N.J.: Prentice-Hall,
1987. 386p., ill., maps, bibl.
   A former diplomatic correspondent, platoon commander in
Sept. 1939, secret army instructor and military attache, now
a historian, Wisconsin's professor gives in this book a
comprehensive overview of Hitler's war. The focus is on the
European theater yet without losing global perspective.
Drawing from the European archival materials, to which
previous historians had no access, the author offers new
insights into the military, strategic and political aspects
of the world conflict. Polish by origin, Dziewanowski makes
sure that Poland's part in the war is not neglected, even if
that part was, in the beginning and end, more that of an
anvil. Many colorful descriptions of battles, military
leaders and statesmen are provided, as well as clandestine
intelligence operations. The language is clear, the material
well organized. "This is history as it ought to be written",
the British reviewer says of the book.

107. _____ . *War at Any Price: World War II in Europe,
1939-1945*. 2nd ed. Englewood Cliffs, N.J.: Prentice-Hall,
1991. 393p., ill. maps, bibl.
   A comprehensive, multifaceted account of World War II
utilizing some of recently available archival records.
Focuses on the war in Europe without neglecting its Far
Eastern connections and attempts to achieve a balance between
the military, diplomatic and psychological aspects of the
world conflict. Some major features of this second, revised
edition include: updated chapter material to discuss recent
political changes in Eastern Europe and Germany and
implications thereof, a few new maps and illustrations never
before published, extended bibliography, and chronology of
military and political events.

108. Jablonski, Edward. *Airwar*. Garden City, N.Y.: Doubleday,
1979. 4 vols.; maps, photos, bibl. (in vol. 4).
   Written with a wide audience in mind, this is a general
account of aerial operations in all theaters of World War II.
Contents of the volumes: 1. "Terror from the Sky"--the
beginning of the war in Poland and Western Europe, with
accent on the Battle of Britain; 2. "Tragic victories"--the
beginnings of the Pacific war and start of the strategic
bombing of Europe; 3. "Outraged Skies"--concerning solely the
Pacific theater; 4. "Wings of Fire"--conclusion of the air

campaigns in the Pacific and European theaters. Numerous
(761) black and white photos.

109. Keegan, John. *The Second World War*. London: Hutchinson,
1989. 608p., ill., maps, portraits, bibl.
    One of the best general histories of WW II ever written.
Contains a two-chapter prologue and sections covering "The
War in the West", "The War in the East" (i.e. the Russo-
German-Balkan war) and "The War in the Pacific."

110. Lipinski, Jerzy. *Druga wojna swiatowa na morzu /The
Second World War at Sea/* 4th ed. Gdansk: Wyd. Morskie, 1976.
863p., plates, ill., maps, tables, bibl.
    An in-depth documentary study of navy operations at the
Second World War Theater, preceded by a detailed political
background of the war. Lists the war participants' navies.
Includes a detailed subject index and numerous maps of
battles.

111. Snyder, Louis Leo. *The War: A Concise History,
1939-1945*. Foreword by Eric Sevareid. New York: Simon and
Schuster, 1960. 579p., ill., maps, bibl.
    This compressed, one-volume popular history of WW II by New
York City College's professor covers all important segments
of the world conflict, while at the same time skillfully
coordinating the reader's view of numerous facts.
Descriptions of military campaigns are included. Emphasis is
placed on the technological and industrial successes of the
Allies, from radar to the A-bomb that helped to win the war.

4b2. German Campaigns

112. Anders, Wladyslaw. *Hitler's Defeat in Russia*. Foreword
by Truman Smith. Chicago: H. Regnery Co., 1953. 267p., maps,
bibl.
    General Anders, commander of forces of Free Poland in the
West during the war, devotes almost one half of work to
Hitler's campaign against Russia in 1941-43. In his polemic
interpretation, he attributes a defeat of the Nazis to their
own ineptitude rather than heroic fighting by the Soviet
Union. Remainder of the book discusses Nazi policy toward
occupied populations and war prisoners, and Western aid to
Russia such as lendlease and bombing of German industry.

113. Berenbrok, Hans Dieter. *The Luftwaffe War Diaries*.
Garden City, NY: Doubleday, 1968. 399p., maps, bibl.
    An interesting German version of the Luftwaffe's part in
the war. Based on official Luftwaffe war diaries, personal
papers of officers, and personal interviews. Covers the
batlles in Poland, the low countries, France, Crete, the
Mediterranean area, Russia and other areas of the European
war theater.

114. Bethell, Nicholas William. *The War Hitler Won: The Fall
of Poland, September 1939*. New York: Holt, Rinehart and
Winston, 1973. 472p., maps, bibl.
    This study provides a thorough analysis and evaluation of
Hitler invasion of Poland in September-October 1939, the

Germans' first full-scale "Blitzkrieg" in the history of war.
The rapidity of its success shocked the Western powers who
expected the Polish army to resist for at least six months.
Bethel criticizes all: the Allies for their failure to act
after their declaration of war on September 3, 1939, American
"neutrality", and Russian complicity.

115. Duffy, Christopher. *Red Storm on the Reich: The Soviet
March on Germany, 1945*. New York: Atheneum: Maxwell Macmillan
International, 1991. 403p., maps, bibl.
   This is a strictly technical history of the final advance
of the Soviet Army, starting with the winter offensive on the
Vistula River in January and ending after the fall of Berlin
in May, 1945. Politics is beyond the scope of this volume.
Duffy, for example, hardly mentions such a fact as Stalin's
lack of support for the Warsaw uprising. Extensively exposed
are casualties inflicted on civilians by the troops of both
armies sweeping over the borderlands.

116. Erickson, John. *The Road to Berlin: Continuing the
History of Stalin's War with Germany*. Boulder, Colo.: Westview
Press, 1983. 877p., ill., maps, bibl.
   This volume presents the story from the collapse of von
Paulus's Sixth Army at Stalingrad to the final days of
fighting through the rubbles of Warsaw, Prague, and Berlin in
May 1945. Military engagements on the Polish land and borders
take many pages of absorbing narration.

117. Guderian, Heinz. *Panzer Leader*. Translated from German
by C. Fitzgibbon. New York: Dutton, 1952. 528p., maps, ill.
   A personalized account of some of the main campaigns in the
European theater by a leading German general. The author
provides a detailed and excellent analysis of the military
aspects of war. Also considers armor tactics. Main focus is
placed on the Blitzkrieg battles of 1939-1940 in Poland and
the west, and the Russian campaigns. Guderian also portrays
Hitler as a military leader and strategist.

118. Halder, Franz. *The Halder Diaries*. 7 vols. Washington:
Infantry Journal, 1950.
   The private diaries of the German Chief of the General
Staff from 1938 to 1942. Provide excellent insights into the
German campaigns in Poland, Norway, France, the Balkans and
Russia which were all successfully completed before Halder's
dismissal in September 1942.

119. Harpur, Brian. *The Impossible Victory: A Personal
Account of the Battle for the River Po*. London: W. Kimber,
1980. 202p., ill., plates.
   A British officer describes the grim realities of Italian
fighting which began at Cassino and continued through the
bitter winter of 1943-44 to the climatic battle in April 1944
which saw the German defenders crumble under ceaseless Allied
attack. On a different level, the author analyzes the
tensions and controversies among the high command on the
basis of postwar interviews with Generals Clark and Wladyslaw
Anders, and Field Marshal Alexander.

120. Kennedy, Robert M. *The German Campaign in Poland, 1939*.
Washington: Dept. of the Army, 1956. 141p., ill., maps, bibl.
(German Report Series, Department of the Army pamphlet no.
20-255).
   "The lessons learned by the German Army in its operations
against Poland were to put to use in the later campaigns
against the western Allies, the Balkan states, and the Soviet
Union." (From the introd.) The purpose of this study by Maj.
Robert Kennedy was to provide the U.S. Army with a factual
account of German military operations against Poland based on
source material from captured records, Dept. of the Army, and
monographs prepared by a number of former German officers for
the Historical Division, U.S. Army, and on such Polish
accounts as available then. This is one of the most competent
and objective works on the subject.

120a. Peszke, Michael Alfred. *Battle for Warsaw, 1939-1944*.
Boulder: East European Monographs; New York: Distributed by
Columbia University Press, 1995.
N.A.

121. Von Mellenthin, Friedrich Wilhelm. *Panzer Battles: A
Study of the Employment of Armor in the Second World War*.
Translated from German by H. Betzler. Norman: University of
Oklahoma Press, 1956. 383p., maps, ill., portraits, bibl.
   An excellent detailed study of the use of armor by the
Germans. The book is divided into four parts: 1. Poland,
France, and the Balkans, 2. The Western Desert, 3. Russia,
and 4. Campaign in the West. The greatest attention is given
to the campaigns in Russia. A number of well done maps help
the reader to interpret the flow of battles and the strategy
of armored warfare. The author was the general and Chief of
Staff of the 4th Panzer Army.

4c. THE POLISH ARMED FORCES IN THE WEST, 1939-1945

122. Anders, Wladyslaw. *An Army in Exile: The Story of the
Second Polish Corps*. With foreword by F. M. Viscount
Alexander of Tunis and introduction by the Rt. Hon. Harold
Macmillan. 1st U.S. ed. Nashville, Tenn.: Battery Press,
1981. 319p, plates, ill, maps, (Allied Forces Series, 1).
Translation of *Bez ostatniego rozdzialu*. Reprint. Orig.
publ.: London: Macmillan, 1949.
   General Anders was the commander of the Second Polish
Corps--the soldiers who planted in blood the Allied flags
atop the Monte Cassino monastery. *An Army in Exile* is in the
first place the General's tribute to his men. But it is more
than that. It is the General's reminiscences of the actions
from 1939 until the dissolution of his corps. This book
belongs in the collection of the basic documents of World War
II.

123. Arct, Bohdan. *Poles against the "V" Weapons*. Translated
from Polish by Beryl Arct. Warsaw: Interpress, 1972. 126p.,
ill., maps, bibl.
   This is an interesting account of Poles' contribution to
fighting V-1 and V-2 unmanned missiles, or "flying
bombs"--Hitler's entirely new and utmost secret weapons.

Those "terror weapons" were to raze London to the ground and force the British Empire to capitulate. The book describes the part played by the Polish Underground Intelligence in sabotage actions which delayed the development and manufacturing of the rockets, as well as raids of British and Polish bomber crews to destroy "V" factories.

124. _____ . *Polish Wings in the West*. Translated from Polish by Beryl Arct. Warszawa: Interpress, 1971. 145p., plates, portraits.
   A book from the popular series "Polish Air Force in the West". Describes the aerial operations after the Polish September disaster, the battle of Britain, air offensives and final victory.

125. Bieganski, Witold. *Poles in the Battle of Narvik*. Translated by Jan Aleksandrowicz. Warszawa: Interpress, 1969. 106p., ill., maps.
   Account of the Polish participation in the Battle of Narvik, May 28-31, 1940. Richly photo-documented.

126. _____ . *Poles in the Battle of Western Europe*. Translated from Polish by Beryl Arct. Warszawa: Interpress, 1971. 158p., ill., bibl.
   Exhibits the Polish contribution to freeing of Europe during the war. Important for numerous illustrations of Polish forces in action in western battles.

127. _____ . *Walki formacji polskich na Zachodzie 1939-1945 /The Struggle of the Polish Military Formations in the West 1939-1945/*. Warszawa: MON, 1981. 835p., plates, ill., portraits, maps, bibl. Summary in English and Russian.
   Presents in a chronological order the struggle of the Polish troops and the diplomatic activity concerning the Polish question during World War II. Includes descriptions of campaigns in the Western Europe, Near East, and North Africa. Well documented.

128. Bohmler, Rudolf. *Monte Cassino*. Translated from German. London: Cassell, 1964. 314p., ill., portraits, maps, bibl.
   A German author examines the Allied attack on Monte Cassino, a key outpost in the Gustav Line, which held a Benedictine abbey that was bombed as a Nazi observatory. Describes the intense fighting which followed the February 15, 1944, air assault and the hill's capture by Polish troops on May 18, 1944.

129. Connell, Charles. *Monte Cassino: The Historic Battle*. London: Elek Books, 1963. 206p., ill., maps, bibl.
   Examines the famous operation in which U.S., French, Polish, and British troops fought for the ruins of the bombed-out Benedictine abbey in May 1944.

130. Harpur, Brian. *The Impossible Victory: A Personal Account of the Battle for the River Po*. London: W. Kimber, 1980. 202p., ill., plates.
   A British officer describes the grim realities of Italian fighting which began at Cassino and continued through the bitter winter of 1943-44 to the climatic battle in April 1944

which saw the German defenders crumble under ceaseless Allied
attack. On a different level, the author analyzes the
tensions and controversies among the high command on the
basis of postwar interviews with Generals Clark and Wladyslaw
Anders, and Field Marshal Alexander.

131. Jordan, Peter. *First to Fight*. Preface by Capt. L.D.
Gammans, M.P. New York: Roy Publishers, 1945. 51p., ill.,
portraits, maps.
A short story describing Poland's invasion by Germany, a
brief account of the struggle, and the aftermath with Polish
forces continuing the struggle overseas.

132. Koniarek, Jan. *Polish Air Force 1939-1945*. New York:
Squadron/Signal Publications, 1994. 64p., ill., photos.
N.A.

133. Lisiewicz, M., ed. *Destiny Can Wait: The Polish Air
Force in the Second World War*. Ed. by M. Lisiewicz.
Translated by A. Truscoe. Foreword by Viscount Portal of
Hungerford. London: William Heinemann, Ltd., 1949. 402p.,
ill., maps.
Story of the Polish Air Force based on combat reports,
squadron diaries and other official records, and on personal
narratives of members of the Air Force. Covers period from
the summer of 1940 through 1945.

134. Meissner, Janusz. *Polish Wings over Europe*. Translated
from Polish by Peter Jordan. Harrow, England: Atlantis
Publishing Co., 1945. 91p., ill.
An outline of the Polish Air Force until 1940.

135. Modelski, Tadeusz. *The Polish Contribution to the
Ultimate Allied Victory in the Second World War*. Worthing,
Sussex: T. Modelski, 1986. 211p., ill., portraits.
"Aimed at telling young people of Polish origin about their
fathers and grandfathers, members of the Polish Armed Forces
in the West during the Second World War: why they came to the
West and what they were doing there." (From the introd.).

136. Piekalkiewicz, Janusz. *Cassino: Anatomy of the Battle*.
London: Orbis, 1980. 192p., ill., facsim., maps, plans,
portraits, bibl. American ed. published under title *The
Battle for Cassino*.
Using documentary evidence, a detailed day-to-day
narrative, and over 150 photographs and maps, the noted
documentary film-maker illuminates the savage, controversial,
and the most frustrating Allied campaign. Shows the
contribution of the Polish II Corps under the command of
General Wladyslaw Anders to the culminating episode of the
battle--conquering Monte Cassino, which was the most
significant Polish victory of the Second World War.

137. Pruszynski, Ksawery. *Poland Fights Back, from
Westerplatte to Monte Cassino*. Translated from Polish by
Peter Jordan, illustr. by Hugo Steiner-Prag. New York: Roy
Publishers, 1944. 191p., ill.
This book is the story of the Poles' unique war record on
land and sea, and in the air--the record of a beaten nation

that kept on fighting. Pruszynski describes the formation of
the Polish army in France after 1939 and follows it through
its adventures and campaigns in France, Great Britain, Norway
and Italy.

138. Rudnicki, Klemens S. *The Last of the War Horses*. London:
Bachman and Turner, 1974. 255p., portraits.
   Story of General Rudnicki and his Polish Army regiments'
"path of destiny" from August 6, 1939 to 1944. The path took
his regiment through the Soviet Russia and eventually through
the Middle East to Italy, France and England.

139. Terlecki, Olgierd. *Poles in the Italian Campaign,
1943-1945*. Translated by Beryl Arct. Warszawa: Interpress,
1972. 136p., ill., maps.
   An account of Polish participation in the Italian campaign.
Numerous black and white illustrations and photographs. One
chapter deals with the Battle of Monte Cassino.

140. Zaloga, Steven J. *The Polish Army, 1939-1945*. London:
Osprey Publishing, 1982. 50p., plates, portraits, bibl.
   A short history of the Polish Army. Of particular value are
colored plates of uniforms of the Army units. Numerous
portraits.

140a. Zamoyski, Adam. *The Forgotten Few: The Polish Air Force
in the Second World War*. New York: Hippocrene Books, 1996.
239p., maps, photos.
   This is not strictly a historical account of the PAF and
its role in the air war on the Allies' side, as the title
would suggest. Based on careful analysis of the official
British and Polish sources, as well as personal narratives of
survivors, this study focuses on the sociological aspects of
the PAF in Great Britain. The author attempts to answer the
questions: who were these men and women?; where did they come
from?; and what did they do? Zamoyski's book is an original
contribution to the literature on the Polish Air Force in the
West.

4d. RESISTANCE AND UNDERGROUND

4d1. European Resistance Movement

141. Foot, Michael Richard Daniel (M R. D.). *Resistance: An
Analysis of European Resistance to Nazism 1940-1945*. London:
Methuen, 1976. 346p., bibl.
   A British historian, who worked with the resistance in
France, provides a panoramic analysis of the resistance
movements in Europe throughout the Second World War. It
covers the whole territory. In the first part of the book the
author explains what resistance was, who resisted, the forms
resistance took, and shows its political problems. The second
part describes a wide spectrum of activities of this
clandestine warfare, country by country.

142. Haestrup, Jorgen. *European Resistance Movements,
1939-1945: A Complete History*. Westport, Conn.: Meckler Pub.,
1981. 564p., maps, bibl.

This is an in-depth comprehensive review of civil
disobedience, intelligence activities, propaganda efforts,
and paramilitary actions in German-occupied countries.
Haestrup demonstrates that the resistance movements were
integral part of the collective conduct of the war.

143. Hoehne, Heinz. *Codeword: Direktor: The Story of the Red
Orchestra*. Translated from German by Richard Barry. New York:
Coward, McCann & Geoghegan, 1971. 310p., bibl.
Hoehne leans very heavily on printed records and archival
materials in this story. The Red Orchestra was a group of
Soviet spies, mostly German informers and Polish Jews, who
operated thoughout Western Europe from 1941 to 1944. The
German author concludes that the Red Orchestra was not a
resistance movement, but traitors who wanted a Soviet
victory. (See also G. Perrault).

144. Juchniewicz, Mieczyslaw. *Poles in the European
Resistance Movement, 1939-1945*. Translated from Polish by
Beryl Arct. Warsaw: Interpress, 1972. 177p., ill., bibl.
Poles joined resistance movements in the occupied countries
of Europe wherever they lived. The book characterizes this
activity in particular parts of the European continent.

145. Michel, Henri. *The Shadow War: European Resistance
1939-1945*. Translated from French by Richard Barry. New York:
Harper & Row, 1973. 416p., bibl.
This well researched study illustrates the development of
the resistance movement in the Nazi occupied areas of Europe.
Traces its origins and shows its position in relation to the
Allies and the occupant's forces. The organization,
strategies and activities of the resistance in different
countries are examined.

4d2. Polish Underground

146. Garlinski, Jozef. *Poland, S.O.E. and the Allies*. London:
Allen and Unwin, 1969. 248p., maps. bibl.
A personal account of the S.O.E.'s Polish Section (one of
national sections of British Special Operations Executives)
by its former agent. The author tells about the training of
Polish agents, secret parachute drops into Poland, organizing
resistance, sabotage, and the development of the Polish Home
Army. There is also material on the various political
problems the English and Poles had with the Russians over the
development and extent of the Polish resistance movement.

147. Gross, Feliks. *The Polish Worker: A Study of Social
Stratum*. Translated by Norbert Guterman. New York: Roy
Publishers, 1945. 274p., bibl.
An analysis of the history and structure of the Polish
labor movement since World War I. Describes the standard of
living of the Polish worker, which was among the lowest in
interwar Europe. A full account of the Nazi treatment of
Polish workers and of the Polish underground struggle is also
added.

148. Karski, Jan. *Story of a Secret State.* London: Houghton, 1944, 391p.
A story of the Polish Underground State told by a young officer who served for more than three years as a liaison between political and military authorities, and as a courier between the Secret State in Poland and the Polish government in exile in London. The Germans were still occupying Warsaw when Karski published his book--perhaps more stressing the author's sensational adventures than realities of the heroic resistance and its dilemmas. Useful as an early chronicle of the Polish resistance, but if you want an exhaustive coverage of the subject, works by Korbonski, Nowak, Zawodny and Lerski are more recommended.

149. Korbonski, Stefan. *Fighting Warsaw: The Story of the Polish Underground State, 1939-1945.* New York: Macmillan, 1956. 495p., ill., portraits, bibl.
A description of the Polish underground movement from 1939 through 1945 by its last head. He portrays the rise and feeling of the Polish national spirit, the conspiratorial atmosphere, and the complicated relations between the Polish government-in-exile in London and the underground leadership in Warsaw. An absorbing account conveying the sense of the resistance in vivid detail.

150. _____. *The Polish Underground State: A Guide to the Underground, 1939-1945.* New York: Columbia University Press, 1978. 268p. (East European Monograph Series, no. 39). Translation of *Polskie panstwo podziemne* by Marta Erdman.
Korbonski has written extensively on politics in Poland during the war. This study will answer most questions on resistance in Poland. Janusz Zawodny's *Nothing but Honor*, an exhaustive study of the Warsaw Uprising, and this work will satisfy most needs for thorough and concise information on this important aspect of World War II.

151. Krakowski, Shmuel. *The War of the Doomed: Jewish Armed Resistance in Poland, 1942-1944.* Holmes & Meyer, 1984. 340p., maps, bibl.
This book deals with Jewish armed resistance in central Poland, which under the occupation was the administrative district known as the Generalgouvernement. An extensive body of sources and literature.

152. Lerski, George "Jur". *Poland's Secret Envoy 1939-1945.* Preface by Stefan Korbonski. New York: Bicentennial Publ Corp, Inc., 1988. 278p., plates, ill., portraits, bibl.
Memoirs of an officer who served the Polish London government during World War II, undertook a risky mission to the Underground State and Home Army in Poland in 1943, and then back to London where he became secretary to Tomasz Arciszewski, the last prime minister. Though mostly an adventure story, the book is more than that due to remarkable primary documentation and bibliographical references. Lerski's account is a useful contribution to the history of the politics and diplomacy of the Polish government-in-exile.

153. Nowak, Jan. *Courier from Warsaw*. Detroit: Wayne State
University Press, 1982. 477p., ill.
   The author was an organizer of propaganda directed to the
German population, and a courier bearing messages to the
Polish authorities abroad and in Warsaw. He returned to
Warsaw to take part in the rising from beginning to end, and
then made another journey to London with messages. Nowak's
detailed account of the 1939-44 period is more than a war
memoir. It is an important contribution to understanding the
Polish sense of nationhood, and the psychology and structure
of the resistance. The book attained immediate popularity in
Poland of the Solidarity era. Complements other treatments in
English of the Polish resistance (e.g. by Korbonski).

154. Poland. Polskie Sily Zbrojne Armia Krajowa. *The Unseen
and Silent: Adventures from the Underground Movement Narrated
by Paratroops of the Polish Home Army*. Translated from Polish
by George Iranek-Osmecki, foreword by Wladyslaw Anders and
Sir Colin Gubbins. London: Sheed and Ward, 1954. 350p., ill.
   Forty studies in which are described the activities of the
Polish paratroops during WW II. They tell about the training
of the troops in Britain, their jumps over Britain, and the
work they did in Poland. "It is a story of the underground
more valuable than most for being seen through many eyes, and
more moving for having no happy ending." (From a review).

155. Studium Polski Podziemnej. *Armia Krajowa w dokumentach
/The Home Army in Documents/*, ed. Halina Czarnocka et al.
London: Studium Polski Podziemnej, 1970-1981. 5 vols., maps.
   Using the archives of the Polish government in London,
"Studium Polski Podziemnej" known in English as the "Polish
Underground Movement (1939-1945) Study Trust", has published
five volumes of documents illustrating the growth of the
Polish Underground State and the Home Army. The documents
provide chronology of events from Sept. 1939 to July 1945.

156. Stypulkowski, Zbigniew. *Invitation to Moscow*. Preface by
H. R. Trevor-Roper. London: Thames and Hudson, 1951. 359p.
   The author, a Polish lawyer and a survivor of the Soviet
Lubianka prison, gives nearly a clinical report on political
terror and other methods used by the Soviets to obtain a
confession of his non-guilt. The book is also important
because Stypulkowski, a Home Army soldier, provides the
detailed story of the Soviet perfidy toward the Polish
underground in the closing days of the Warsaw uprising.

157. Tenenbaum, Joseph Leib. *Underground: The Story of a
People*. New York: Philosophical Library, 1952. 532p., ill.,
bibl.
   Annotated, with a bibliography and index, this is a
detailed description of the mass extermination of Jews in
Poland under Nazi tyranny. Much material deals with the
Jewish underground and battle for the Warsaw Ghetto.

4d3. The Warsaw Uprising, 1944 (for the Warsaw Ghetto Uprising, see 7c3. The Holocaust)

158. Bor-Komorowski, Tadeusz. *The Secret Army*. Nashville: Battery Press, 1984. 407p., ill., maps. bibl. (The Allied Forces Series, no. 2). 1st U.S. ed. New York: Macmillan, 1951.
   The explicit account of the Warsaw Uprising by one of the organizers of the Polish underground movement and the Commander-in-chief of the Polish Home Army.

159. Bruce, George Ludgate. *The Warsaw Uprising, 1 August–2 October 1944*. London: Hart-Davis, 1972. 224p., ill., map, portraits, bibl.
   Presents the story of the Warsaw Uprising of 1 August 1944 and also gives some idea of the policies and of the people responsible for the events which made a heap of rubble out of one of Europe's finest cities, and killed some 250,000 people. The book not only shows a drama of unexampled heroism ending in appalling tragedy, but also provides the reader with the first example of full-scale urban guerilla warfare. Covers in detail the growth, training and development of the Secret Army, as well as the motives which inspired it. To achieve the purpose of his work, the author has turned to the official documents of the wartime Polish government-in-exile and some published documents and interviews. A companion volume to the studies of Bor-Komorowski, Ciechanowski and Zawodny.

160. Ciechanowski, Jan. *Powstanie warszawskie: zarys podloza politycznego i dyplomatycznego /The Warsaw Uprising: An Outline of the Political and Diplomatic Background/*. London: Odnova Ltd, 1971. 397p., bibl. Summary in English.
   The Polish wartime ambassador to Washington (1941–45), Ciechanowski has published a critical study based on his PhD dissertation at the London School of Economics and Political Sciences, 1968. Considers political and ideological factors, as well as the course of events and causes that led to the outbreak of the Warsaw uprising.

161. _____ . *The Warsaw Rising of 1944*. London, New York: Cambridge University Press, 1974. 332p., map, bibl. (Soviet & East European Studies series).
   A revised and abridged version of the author's PhD thesis, *The Political and Ideological Background of the Warsaw Rising, 1944* submitted to the London School of Economics and Political Sciences, 1968, and of the Polish edition published in 1971 under title: *Powstanie warszawskie: zarys podloza politycznego i dyplomatycznego*.

162. Hanson, Joanna K. M. *The Civilian Population and the Warsaw Uprising of 1944*. Cambridge: Cambridge University Press, 1982. 345p., ill., bibl.
   Based on the author's doctoral dissertation at the University of London in 1978, this book shows the desperate conditions of civilian life in Warsaw during the two-month-long military uprising. Traces in detail the course of the uprising. Hanson complements the previous studies on the subject by Bruce, Ciechanowski, Korbonski, and Zawodny.

163. Orpen, Neil D. *Airlift to Warsaw: The Rising of 1944*.
Norman, Okla: University of Oklahoma Press, 1984. 184p.,
maps, ill., bibl.
  In August 1944, when the Germans rushed in SS troops, the
Home Army seized the control of the city. Soviet Armies,
which were driving into Warsaw, stopped to await the outcome.
Then Churchill ordered British, South African and Polish
elements of the Allied Balkan Air Force to mount a supply
airlift to Warsaw. This is a reconstruction of a number of
those missions, doomed as the uprising itself. Losses were
heavy. *Am Hist Rev* regards Orpen's accounts as "the best
descriptions of night bomber flying in the entire World War
II literature".

164. Zagorski, Waclaw. *Seventy Days*. London: Muller, 1957.
267p., ill., portraits, maps, bibl.
  The daily story from July 30 to October 7, 1944 of the
uprising and struggles of the Polish Home Army in the battle
to rid Warsaw of German troops upon the approach of Soviet
forces. Despite assurances of Soviet aid and support, the
Soviet troops stopped at the Vistula River which was all that
separated them from the fighting Poles. This abandoned the
Home Army, and its potential postwar source of Polish
leadership, to an aroused and reinforced German force.

165. Zawodny, Janusz Kazimierz. *Nothing but Honor: The Story
of the Warsaw Uprising, 1944*. Stanford, Calif.: Hoover
Institution, 1978. 328p., ill., bibl. (Hoover Institution
Publication, 183).
  A participant in the 1944 Warsaw uprising and author of
Death in the Forest, an inquiry into the Katyn massacre,
Zawodny comes with the definitive and comprehensive account
of a crucial event in World War II. Many studies of the
uprising have appeared. Zawodny's bibliography encompasses
them all to 1978. Appendixes contain comparative statistics,
interviews with General Bor, head of the Polish underground's
Home Army, and George Kennan, as well as a list of 72 persons
interviewed by the author. On the vexed question of Soviet
failure to resume their offensive during the 63 days of
fighting, Zawodny sides with those who consider this a
political decision, although he acknowledges that Soviet
archives, unavailable for western scholars, may contain
materials that would force a revision of this judgement.

4e. MILITARY INTELLIGENCE AND CLANDESTINE OPERATIONS

166. Arct, Bohdan. *Poles against the "V" Weapons*. Translated
from Polish by Beryl Arct. Warsaw: Interpress, 1972. 126p.,
ill., maps, bibl.
  This is an interesting account of Poles' contribution to
fighting V-1 and V-2 unmanned missiles, or "flying bombs"--
Hitler's entirely new and utmost secret weapons. Those
"terror weapons" were to raze London to the ground and force
the British Empire to capitulate. The book describes the part
played by the Polish Underground Intelligence in sabotage
actions which delayed the development and manufacturing of
the rockets, as well as raids of British and Polish bomber
crews to destroy "V" factories.

167. Garlinski, Jozef. *Hitler's Last Weapons: The Underground War against the V1 and V2*. New York: Times Books, 1978. 244p., plates, ill., bibl.
   Dr. Garlinski has used British, German, Polish, French, Danish, Dutch, and Jewish archives and published works, and consulted survivors, to survey in this exciting book the intelligence operations of agents and resistance figures from these countries who sought to uncover and relay to London the secrets of the Nazi revenge-weapons, pilotless aircrafts V1 and V2.

168. _____. *Poland, S.O.E. and the Allies*. London: Allen and Unwin, 1969. 248p., maps. bibl.
   A personal account of the S.O.E.'s Polish Section (one of national sections of British Special Operations Executives) by its former agent. The author tells about the training of Polish agents, secret parachute drops into Poland, organizing resistance, sabotage, and the development of the Polish Home Army. There is also material on the various political problems the English and Poles had with the Russians over the development and extent of the Polish resistance movement.

169. _____. *The Swiss Corridor: Espionage Networks in Switzerland during World War II*. London: Dent, 1981. 222p., plates, ill., maps, facsims, portraits, bibl.
   Since the archives concerning the intelligence services operating in the "actively neutral Switzerland" during World War II are still closed, Garlinski had to rely in this book on witnesses, fragmentary information, and only on the few original sources. Given these limitations, the author concentrates on the most important topics and informs a wide audience, not only specialists, mainly of Swiss, Soviet, American, British, and German intelligence activities. Polish, French, Italian, Czechoslovak and Austrian achievements are also "brought into the picture".

170. Gondek, Leszek. *Dzialalnosc Abwehry na terenie Polski, 1933-1939 /Abwehr Operations in Poland, 1933-1939/*. 2nd ed. Warszawa: Wyd. MON, 1974. 354p., ill., bibl.
   Based on a variety of Polish and foreign sources, this in-depth study gives a comprehensive picture of Abwehr--Hitler's military intelligence and its operations in interwar Poland. Concludes with assessment of future results of those activities for Poland.

171. Hoehne, Heinz. *Codeword: Direktor: The Story of the Red Orchestra*. Translated from German by Richard Barry. New York: Coward, McCann & Geoghegan, 1971. 310p., bibl.
   Hoehne leans very heavily on printed records and archival materials in this story. The Red Orchestra was a group of Soviet spies, mostly German informers and Polish Jews, who operated thoughout Western Europe from 1941 to 1944. The German author concludes that the Red Orchestra was not a resistance movement, but traitors who wanted a Soviet victory. (See also G. Perrault).

172. Jong, Louis De. *The German Fifth Column in the Second World War*. Translated from Dutch by C.M. Geyl. Chicago: University of Chicago Press, 1956. 308p., maps, bibl.

This is a very absorbing monograph. Through country after
country: Poland, France, Norway, Denmark, the Netherlands,
Belgium, England, the United States and South America--this
carefully documented study traces the German Fifth Column
activity throughout the world, to show in conclusion the myth
and the reality behind the myth.

173. Leverkuehn, Paul. *German Military Intelligence*. New
York: Praeger, 1954. 209p., maps.
    A personalized account of Abwehr operations in the Balkans,
Russia, Poland and Western Europe. The most effective parts
of the book tell of Nazi interference which made the Abwehr
under Admiral Canaris an ineffective organization.

174. Lewin, Ronald. *Ultra Goes to War: The Secret Story*.
London: Hutchinson, 1978. 397p., bibl.
    Examines *Ultra*, the method by which the Allies intercepted
German radio transmissions and broke their coded contents.
Credits the contribution of Polish mathematicians to the
breaking of the Enigma code. Describes a practical
application of Ultra and Enigma in combat.

175. Listowell, Judith M. H. *Crusades in the Secret War*.
London: Christopher Johnson, 1952. 287p.
    Relation of the story of Col. Nart, a Polish-born secret
agent, and his dealings with Germans' satellite intelligence
services. Some fragments concerned with Poland.

176. Perrault, Giles. *The Red Orchestra*. Translated by Peter
Wiles. New York: Simon and Schuster, 1969. 496p., bibl.
    This work is the story of the Russian spy network, the Red
Orchestra, which operated against the Germans in occupied
France, Belgium, and Holland from 1941 to 1944. The leader
was a Polish Jew, Leopold Trepper, who directed the flow of
information over clandestine radio links with Moscow. The
author has been able to talk with many of the survivors,
including Trepper (See also H. Hoehne).

177. Poland. Ministerstwo Informacji. *The German Fifth Column
in Poland*. London: Hutchinson and Co., Ltd., 1947. 157p.,
maps, ill.
    Based on primary documents and eyewitness accounts, this
fascinating book reveals the operations of the German spies
and diversionist agents in Poland. Shows the Nazi subversive
methods which also were used in other occupied countries.

178. Poland. Polskie Sily Zbrojne Armia Krajowa. *The Unseen
and Silent: Adventures from the Underground Movement Narrated
by Paratroops of the Polish Home Army*. Translated from Polish
by George Iranek-Osmecki, foreword by Wladyslaw Anders and
Sir Colin Gubbins. London: Sheed and Ward, 1954. 350p., ill.
    Forty studies in which are described the activities of the
Polish paratroops during World War II. They tell about the
training of the troops in Britain, their jumps over Britain,
and the work they did in Poland. "It is a story of the
underground more valuable than most for being seen through
many eyes, and more moving for having no happy ending."(From
a review).

179. Tickell, Jerrard. *Moon Squadron.* New York: Doubleday,
1958. 204p.
An absorbing account of the Special Operations Executive
(SOE), a secret military organization set up in London in
1940. The two better known groups were 138 and 161 Squadrons
composed of both British and Polish flyers. Their activities
included transporting Allied undercover agents to and from
England, supplying Polish and other resistance organizations
with arms and provisions, and carrying out special bombing
missions over Poland and other occupied countries.

180. Wood, E. Thomas, and Stanislaw M. Jankowski. *Karski: How
One Man Tried to Stop the Holocaust.* Foreword by Elie Wiesel.
New York: John Wiley, 1994. 316p., plates, ill., map, bibl.
The authors' goal was to present a chronological and
factual account of Jan Karski's wartime activities. The book
recounts the Polish Army officer's heroic and exciting
escapades: Nazi and Soviet imprisonment, escapes, his service
as a secret agent for the Polish underground. Focus is on
Karski's struggles as a diplomatic courier to aid the Home
Army, and to inform the world's VIPs about the Nazi
atrocities in the Warsaw Ghetto and elsewhere. His testimony
was not taken seriously. "Some refused to listen to him,
others to believe him", points out E. Wiesel in the foreword.
Based on Karski's oral reminiscences and extensive reading of
Polish and foreign materials, this biography of the young
Polish Catholic is valuable, for it tempers the wide-spread
contention that Gentle Poland was indifferent to the plight
of the Jews. (See also Karski-author in this bibliography.)

4e1. The Enigma Code-Breaking Machine

181. Garlinski, Jozef. *The Enigma War.* New York: Charles
Scribner's Sons, 1980. 255p., bibl.   British edition
published under title: *Intercept.*
Presents the history and methods of breaking up and
reconstructing the German ciphering machine Enigma by the
cryptographic section of the Intelligence Service of the
Polish Army soon before the outbreak of World War II. Plates,
drawings, photographs, and diagrams of the system.

182. _____ . *Poland in the Second World War.* New York:
Hippocrene Books, 1985. 508p., plates, maps, portraits, bibl.
The author of numerous popular accounts on various aspects
of the war, Garlinski in this book has skillfully compressed
a mass of information based on western, eastern, and even
Vatican sources to present a one-volume documentary history
of Poland's involvement in World War II. He seeks to treat
"Polish affairs in the context of larger global political and
military concerns." Garlinski also discusses the Enigma.

183. Kahn, David. *Kahn on Codes: Secrets of the New
Cryptology.* New York: Macmillan, 1983. 343p., bibl.
David Kahn is America's foremost authority on codes,
ciphers, and spies. Here in chapter "The Spy Who Most
Affected World War II", the author tells an interesting and
carefully documented story of the German spy who delivered
documents that enabled the Polish cryptanalysts to solve and

reconstruct the German army's Enigma cipher machine. The
solution achieved by the Poles led to what has rightly been
called the most important sustained intelligence success in
the human conflict (p 88).

184. Kozaczuk, Wladyslaw. *Enigma: How the German Machine
Cipher Was Broken, and How It Was Read by the Allies on World
War Two*. 1st U.S. ed. Frederick, Md: University Publications
of America, 1984. 362p., plates, ill., bibl. Translation of
the Polish version (1979): *W kregu Enigmy* by C. Kasperek.
  Based on published and unpublished Polish and foreign
sources, this book documents the Polish contribution to the
breaking of the Enigma code, both prior to the invasion and
after. Records the assistance by the Polish codebreakers to
the British with the Ultra. The role of the Ultra program in
the main European battles is recounted.

185. Lewin, Ronald. *Ultra Goes to War: The Secret Story*.
London: Hutchinson, 1978. 397p., bibl.
  Examines *Ultra*, the method by which the Allies intercepted
German radio transmissions and broke their coded contents.
Credits the contribution of Polish mathematicians to the
breaking of the Enigma code. Describes a practical
application of Ultra and Enigma in combat.

186. Winterbotham, Frederick William. *The Ultra Secret*. *1st
U.S. ed.* New York: Harper & Row, 1974. 199p.
  An account of the British secret service officer
responsible for running the project. Tells how the
intelligence service penetrated the Germans' most secret
cipher machine called Enigma, and how such material as could
be gleaned from this source was sent out to, and used by, the
combined chiefs of staff. Due credit is given to the "Polish
genesis" of the project. Winterbotham wrote from memory,
therefore his book is inaccurate, careless about the facts
and dates.

187. Woytak, Richard A. *On the Border of War and Peace:
Polish Intelligence and Diplomacy in 1937-1939 and the
Origins of the Ultra Secret*. New York: Columbia University
Press, 1979. 141p., ill., bibl.
  This short book with a lengthy title covers the two last
years of peace. It surveys Polish efforts to secure its
interests in the forthcoming crisis. Deals more with
diplomacy than with intelligence, and the connection between
the two is not clearly apparent. Woytak overstates the role
of both, but provides useful background facts on Poland's
role in developing the Enigma code-breaking machine.
Extensive bibliography.

5
POLITICAL AND DIPLOMATIC ASPECTS OF THE WAR

5a. ALLIED WARTIME DIPLOMACY (see also 8a. Big Three Wartime Conferences)

188. Batowski, Henryk. *Wojna a dyplomacja, 1945 /War and Diplomacy, 1945/*. Poznan: Wydawn. Poznanskie, 1972. 348p., ill., bibl. Summary in English and Russian.
   Covers the diplomatic activities of the anti-fascist coalition in the final stages of the war, from January 1945 to September 1945. The main goal of those official and non-official negotiations was (a) to prepare the groundwork for the capitulation of the German and Japanese forces, and (b) the formulation of a new political system in East Central Europe, with the Soviet Union as the focal point. Cites many western sources.

189. Fischer, Louis. *The Road to Yalta: Soviet Foreign Relations, 1941-1945*. New York: Harper and Row, 1972. 238p., bibl.
   This well documented study surveys the wartime relations between Soviet Russia and its allies, the United States and Britain. Considerable space is devoted to Poland which the author sees as the main component of the Soviet expansionist policies and the key to Stalin's control of Europe.

190. Gilbert, Martin. *Auschwitz and the Allies*. London: M. Joseph/Reinbird, 1981. 368p., plates, maps, portraits, bibl.
   An account of when and how the Allies learned of Nazi atrocities against Jewish population and of their reaction. Emphasis on England and its respose to Hitler's attempted destruction of Europe's Jews.

191. Jedrzejewicz, Waclaw. *Poland in the British Parliament, 1939-1945*. New York: Jozef Pilsudski Institute of America, 1946-1962. 3 vols., maps, bibl.
   Stenographic reports of Parliamentary debates on Anglo-Polish relations from March 3, 1939 through July 1945. Explanatory notes precede the documents. Volumes 2 and 3 include material relating to Poland gathered from other

sources as well, but on the general topic.

192. Koenig, Louis William. *The Presidency and the Crisis*.
New York: Columbia University Press, 1944. 166p., bibl.
    A study of the presidential power. It specifically covers
the period from the invasion of Poland to Pearl Harbor, and
is concerned particularly with foreign relations, military
affairs and the home front. Contemporary history has
witnessed considerable expansion of the executive power. That
development may call for an immediate response to the demands
of the Machtpolitik and justify the use of force by a
political state in the attainment of its objectives. A
leisurely diplomacy has no place in a totalitarian era, the
author suggests.

193. Lukas, Richard C. *The Strange Allies: The United States
and Poland, 1941-1945*. Knoxville: University of Tennessee
Press, 1978. 230p., maps, bibl.
    This is a "history of U.S. wartime relations with Poland,
the Polish government in exile, Poland's military forces in
the west, and her legion detained in the Soviet Union..."
Concluding that "there was always more sympathy than support
for Poland in the United States during the war", Lukas sets
forth the main lines of American policy, from Roosevelt's
quest for Polish ethnic votes to the complexities of trying
to persuade Stalin to release Poland.

194. Maisky, Ivan Mikhailovich. *Memoirs of a Soviet
Ambassador: The War 1939-43*. Translated from Russian by
Andrew Rothstein. New York: Scribner, 1968. 408p., bibl.
    This book by the Soviet ambassador to Great Britain from
1932 deals with his experiences during World War II from the
start of Hitler's invasion of Poland to September 1943 when
Stalin recalled Maisky to Moscow as an expression of his
disappointment with the Allied postponement of a second front
in Europe. The narrative gives an assessment of wartime
Soviet-Allied diplomatic relations. The reader also learns
about the way Maisky manipulated London's and other western
leaders and about Stalin's dilemmas with various East
European governments-in-exile based in London.

195. McSherry, James E. *Stalin, Hitler and Europe: The
Imbalance of Power, 1939-1941*. Cleveland, Ohio: World
Publishing Co., 1970. 357p., bibl.
    The discussion covers the time between the German invasion
of Poland and that of Soviet Russia. Focuses on the
interaction between Hitler and Stalin in the context of
squeezing smaller states, such as Poland and Romania, between
the two. Useful as a contribution to the diplomatic history
of the eve of the German-Soviet war. The author criticizes
both Hitler and Stalin for a lack of understanding of each
other's motives.

196. Perlmutter, Amos. *FDR and Stalin. A Not So Grand
Alliance, 1943-1945*. Columbia, Miss: University of Missouri
Press, 1993. 331p., maps, ill., bibl.
    With the dissolution of the Soviet Union, historians are
now capable of examining the evolution of U.S.-Soviet
relations from Moscow's perspective. Based on Soviet archival

sources as well as the materials of the Roosevelt library, this study re-interprets the roles of Stalin and Roosevelt in creating the Russo-American alliance, at the cost of others. Large fragments concern the Polish question. Here Perlmutter describes Soviet Embassy papers reporting FDR's domestic pressures (from American Catholics and the Polish ethnic minority, which were seen by Gromyko as the most anti-Soviet group) that the Russians thought might impede their plans for Poland. On this point, the author repeats known facts from 1939 to 1945 and the Yalta "sellouts".

197. Zochowski, Stanislaw. *British Policy in Relation to Poland in the Second World War*. New York: Vintage Press, 1988. 207p., bibl.
N.A.

5b. POLISH DIPLOMACY IN EXILE, 1939-1945 (see also 8al. The Polish Question)

198. Batowski, Henryk. *Z dziejow dyplomacji polskiej na obczyznie: wrzesien 1939-lipiec 1941. /Polish Diplomacy in Exile (1939-1941)/*. Krakow: Wydawn. Literackie, 1984. 453p., leaves, plates, ill., portraits, maps., bibl. Summaries in English, French and German.
Discusses the goals pursued by Polish foreign policy in the years 1939-1941 under the direction of Wladyslaw Sikorski, Premier of the Polish government-in-exile. The balance of this diplomatic activity is recognized as positive, despite some errors.

199. Ciechanowski, Jan. *Defeat in Victory*. Garden City, N.Y.: Doubleday, 1947. 397p., bibl.
Polish ambassador to the United States describes wartime negotiations with the U.S. and other Allied governments on behalf of the Polish government-in-exile. With his feelings under control, Ciechanowski denounces the evasions and hipocrisy of diplomacy in the transcripts of secret talks with the leaders of the Big Three. The author participated in many of the related events. Enhanced by texts of diplomatic reports, and official records.

200. Engel, David. *Facing a Holocaust: The Polish Government in Exile and the Jews, 1943-1945*. Chapel Hill: University of North Carolina Press, 1993. 317p., bibl.
Examines the relations between the government in exile, its representatives and diplomats all over the world, and different leaders and officials of the Jewish organizations active at the time.

201. General Sikorski Historical Institute. *Documents on Polish-Soviet Relations, 1939-1945*. Vol. 2, *1943-1945*. Ed. Edward Raczynski and others. London: Humanities Press, 1968. 868p.
This important collection of some 400 documents on the relations between the Soviet government and Polish government in exile covers the period of May 1943 to August 1945, when after the resolutions of the Potsdam Conference the recognition of the Polish government in London was withdrawn

by the Western Allies. It also contains much information
about Allied policy in reshaping the political map of Eastern
Europe.

202. Gross, Feliks. *Crossroads of Two Continents: A
Democratic Federation of East-Central Europe*. New York:
Columbia University Press, 1945. 162p., maps, bibl.
  A federal solution to the problems of central and east
Europe had its strong advocates, to name such figures as
Thomas Masaryk, Edward Benes, and Gen. Sikorski. The idea
gained a considerable interest among some groups of exile
governments in London. Based on wide research, this study
presents the plans, current in the first years of the war,
with respect to the "crossroads of two continents--the region
of east-central Europe". (See also Wandycz, *Czechoslovak-
Polish Confederation*).

203. Instytut Polski, and Muzeum Sikorskiego. *General
Sikorski, premier, naczelny wodz /General Sikorski, Prime
Minister, Commander in Chief/*. Photographs selected by Regina
Oppman; text by Bohdan Wronski; designed by Juliusz L.
Englert. London: Polish Institute and Sikorski Museum in
London, 1981. 130p., ill. Text in English and Polish.
  The album intended as "a tribute to the memory of General
Sikorski, a leading statesman and an outstanding soldier in
the service of his country and the cause of freedom -- on the
occasion of the one hundredth anniversary of his birth. The
album depicts his most active and fruitful years and covers
the period from the end of September 1939 until his untimely
death at Gibraltar in July 1943." Index of names. This is a
valuable contribution to the history of the politics and
diplomacy of the Polish government in exile.

204. Irving, David J. C. *Accident: The Death of General
Sikorski*. London: William Kimber, 1967.231p., ill., maps,
notes and sources.
  The story about the events surrounding the fatal airplane
crash which cost the life of General Wladyslaw Sikorski.
Numerous illustrations. Well documented to suggest that the
crash was more than just an accident.

205. Kacewicz, George V. *Great Britain, the Soviet Union, and
the Polish Goernment in Exile (1939-1945)*. The Hague; Boston:
M. Nijhoff, 1979. 255p., bibl. (Studies in Contemporary
History, vol. 3).
  George V. Kacewicz of California State University writes
with sympathy for the Polish government-in-exile, which can
hardly be blamed for refusing to give up half of Poland
without the population being consulted and without guarantees
for either adequate compensation or postwar independence. He
criticizes both Stalin's ruthlessness and the policy of
concessions toward him adopted first by the British and then
by the American government. The author states that no matter
what the Polish government might have done, the final outcome
could hardly have been different.

206. Korpalska, Walentyna. *Wladyslaw Sikorski, biografia
polityczna /Wladyslaw Sikorski: A Political Biography/*.
Wroclaw: Ossol. 1981. 263p., ill., plates, portraits, bibl.

A scholarly, "authentic biographical account" of General Wladyslaw Sikorski, Commander-in-Chief and Premier of the Polish government-in-exile. Traces the evolution of his political and socio-economic views. Seeks to reconstruct the process of making his legend and confront it with realities. The author cites an unusually rich collection of primary and secondary sources, enhanced by numerous personalia and authorized personal narratives.

207. Kot, Stanislaw. *Conversations with the Cremlin, and Dispatches from Russia*. Translated from Polish by H.C. Stevens. London: Oxford University Press, 1963. 285p.
    Chiefly translations of reports of various conversations held by the author with various members of the Soviet government while ambassador to Russia from Poland during the period of 4 September 1941 to 13 July 1942. Also contains translations of other reports to General Sikorski.

208. Lerski, George "Jur". *Poland's Secret Envoy 1939-1945*. Preface by Stefan Korbonski. New York: Bicentennial Publ Corp, Inc., 1988. 278p., plates, ill., portraits, bibl.
    Memoirs of an officer who served the Polish London government during World War II, undertook a risky mission to the Underground State and Home Army in Poland in 1943, and then back to London where he became secretary to Tomasz Arciszewski, the last prime minister. Though mostly an adventure story, the book is more than that due to remarkable primary documentation and bibliographical references. Lerski's account is a useful historical account of the politics and diplomacy of the Polish government-in-exile.

208a. Piotrowski, Thaddeus M. *Polish-Ukrainian Relations during World War II: Ethnic Cleansing in Volhynia and Eastern Galicia*. Toronto: Adam Mickiewicz Foundation, 1995. N.A.

209. Prazmowska, Anita. *Britain and Poland, 1939-1943: The Betrayed Ally*. Cambridge, New York: Cambridge University Press, 1995. (Soviet and European Studies, vol. 97). N.A.

210. Raczynski, Edward. *In Allied London*. London: Polish Research Centre, 1960. 450p., ill., portraits, bibl.
    The WW II memoirs of the Polish Ambassador to London and the subsequent Polish Minister for Foreign Affairs. Narrates events as seen through Polish eyes of the fortunes of Poland at war. Describes the political situation during its invasion, Poland's combat role from Britain, the political problems of dealing with the Big Three with their divergent viewpoints and policies, up to the final Allied withdrawal of recognition for the Polish government in exile.

211. Sword, Keith, ed. *Sikorski: Soldier and Statesman*. London: Orbis Books, 1990. 224p., plates, ill., maps, portraits, bibl. (SSEES Occasional Papers; no. 8).
    A collection of essays written by British and Polish historians for the topical symposium held at the School of Slavonic and East European Studies, University of London, September 26-27, 1983.

212. Terry, Sarah Meiklejohn. *Poland's Place in Europe:
General Sikorski and the Origin of the Oder-Neisse Line,
1939-1943*. Princeton, N.J.: Princeton University Press, 1983.
394p., maps, bibl.

The Oder-Neisse line, since 1945 the boundary between
Poland and Germany, has long been seen as the product of
Communist policy. On the basis of extensive research in U.S.
and European archives, Terry challenges this view. Focusing
on the early years of World War II, rather than on the period
between the conferences of Teheran and Potsdam, she attempts
to show that the design of shifting Polish boundaries
westward was originally devised by General Wladyslaw
Sikorski, Prime Minister of the Polish government-in-exile,
1939-1943. She concludes that Sikorski considered the
boundary changes part of a larger security plan, which also
included a Central European federation of small states (see
Gross and Wandycz). Other issues related to Sikorski's
policies are explored.

213. Umiastowski, Roman. *Poland, Russia and Great Britain,
1941-1945: A Study of Evidence*. London: Hollis and Carter,
1946. 544p., maps, bibl.

Covers the relations between Poland and Russia on the one
hand, and between Poland and Britain on the other, during a
period of four years beginning from the Russo-Polish Treaty
of 1941 and the Yalta Agreement, and the recognition by the
Allies in July 1945 of the Soviet-sponsored Lublin Committee
as the Polish Provisional Government. Well documented.

214. Wandycz, Piotr Stefan. *Czechoslovak-Polish Confederation
and the Great Powers, 1940-1943*. Bloomington: Indiana
University Press, 1956. 152p., bibl. (Slavic and East
European Series, vol. 3).

Describes the proposed post-war confederation between the
two countries as discussed by their London-based governments-
in-exile. The ultimate goal of this union was to come to a
common policy with regard to foreign affairs, defense, and
economic, financial, and social matters. The abandonment of
the negotiations was due, in large part, to Soviet pressures
and the desire of the two nations to maintain friendly
relations with Soviet Russia.

214a. Waszak, Leon J. *Agreement in Principle: The Wartime
Partnership of General Wladyslaw Sikorski and Winston
Churchill*. New York: P. Lang, 1996.
N.A.

215. Zajdlerowa, Zoe. *The Dark Side of the Moon*. London:
Faber, 1946. 299p.

An account of Polish-Soviet relations 1939-45 from the
standpoint of Soviet actions as a result of the 1939 pact
between Germany and the Soviet Union and the subsequent
Soviet occupation of the eastern part of Poland. Describes
the imposition of the Soviet pattern of life upon the Poles
and the resultant consequences.

6
ECONOMIC AND LEGAL ASPECTS OF THE WAR

216. Ordon, Stanislaw. *Wojna obronna Polski w 1039 roku na wybrzezu in morzu w swietle prawa miedzynarodowego /Poland's War of Defense on the Coast and at Sea in 1939, in the Light of International Law.* Gdansk: Ossolineum, 1974. 361p., ill., bibl. Summaries in English, German and Russian.
Analyzes the preparations made by the Third Reich to invade Poland, and the criminal activities of the German armed forces on the Polish coast and at sea in 1939, from the point of view of international law.

217. Polomski, Franciszek. *Aspekty rasowe w postepowaniu z robotnikami przymusowymi i jencami wojennymi III Rzeszy, 1939-1945 /Racial aspects in the Treatment of Compulsory Workers in the Third Reich/.* Wroclaw: Ossolineum, 1976. 130p., bibl. Summary in English.
Deals with Nazi racism in practice. Discusses restrictions, prohibitions and sanctions resulting from racist doctrines applied to conscript labor and prisoners of war in the Third Reich. Based predominantly on materials from Polish and German archives.

218. Prazmowska, Anita. *Britain, Poland, and the Eastern Front, 1939.* Cambridge: Cambridge University Press, 1987. 231p., bibl., (Soviet and East European Studies)
This is a persuasive scholarly interpretation of the implications and consequences of Britain's inability to forge an Eastern front against Germany. Prazmowska's study includes a thorough analysis and evaluation of both economic policy and military planning for this front. She concludes by exploring the implications of this failure, especially with reference to Poland.

7

SOCIAL IMPACT OF THE WAR

7a. OCCUPATION, GERMAN AND SOVIET

7a1. General Accounts

219. Lukas, Richard C. *The Forgotten Holocaust: The Poles under German Occupation, 1939-1944*. Lexington, Ky: University Press of Kentucky, 1986. 300p., plates, ill., bibl.
A study of Polish suffering under the German occupation in World War II based on interviews and Polish archival sources, as well as published material. Discusses the military underground, civilian resistance and collaboration, the Warsaw uprising, and the relations between Poles and Jews. He asserts that the killing of three million non-Jewish Poles by the Nazis is "an event comparable to what is now generally designated by the word 'holocaust', i.e. the systematic Nazi attempt to kill Europe's Jews."

220. Poland. Ministerstwo Informacji. *Black Book of Poland: German New Order in Poland*. New York: Putnam, 1942. 615p., ill., maps.
Compiled under the auspices of the Polish Ministry of Information. This massive collection of documents, statements, letters, photographs, and personal histories provides a precise record of the Nazi New Order as applied to a conquered country. It shows exactly how the Nazis attempted to destroy the spirit, culture, religions, and the bodies of the nation. Covers only the period from September 1939 to July 1941. Names, photographs, maps, statistics, and depositions.

221. Polskie Towarzystwo Naukowe na Obczyźnie. *Napasc sowiecka i okupacja polskich ziem wschodnich (wrzesien 1939): praca zbiorowa pod auspicjami Polskiego Towarzystwa Naukowego na Obczyźnie /The Soviet Aggression and Occupation of the Polish Eastern Territories (September 1939)/*, ed. Jozef Jasnowski, Edward Szczepanik. London: Polish Cultural Foundation, 1985. 112p., plates, ill., maps, bibl.
On Sept. 17, 1939, when Poland was engaged in the defense

against Hitler's aggression, the Soviets invaded her eastern
territories. This documentary study addresses historical,
political, and strategic aspects, as well as the course of
military actions and direct consequencies of the Soviet
invasion.

222. Segal, Simon. *Nazi Rule in Poland*. London: Robert Hale,
Ltd., 1945. 214p., ill., maps, bibl. General Gouvernement.
   An attempt to describe in scientific detail Nazi rule in
Poland. Nazis were deporting and exterminating Poles in order
to make a new living space (Lebensraum) for German colonists.
Covers organization of the regime, population, religious,
cultural and economic life, ghettos, and the Underground
Movement. Map of interwar Poland delineating areas
incorporated into Germany and General Gouvernment.

223. Sword, Keith, ed. *The Soviet Takeover of the Polish
Eastern Provinces, 1939-41*. New York: St. Martin's Press,
1991. 318p., maps, bibl.
   A collection of papers delivered at a conference held at
the School of Slavonic and East European Studies, University
of London, in April 1989 to mark the fiftieth anniversary of
the Soviet takeover of eastern Poland. The conference was
convened in order to bring together scholars from both inside
and outside Poland interested in the subject. The papers
provided express the diverse interests and concerns of their
authors.

224. Wright, Gordon. *The Ordeal of Total War, 1939-1945*. New
York: Harper & Row, 1968. 315p., ill., maps, bibl. (The Rise
of Modern Europe series, 20).
   A variety of areas are covered in this study of Europe
during the war. Explores the economic, psychological,
cultural and scientific impacts of the struggle, discusses
Germany's plans for consolidating its conquests after the
occupation of Poland, the Soviet Union, and the rest of the
European continent, and analyzes Europe's response to
conquest, which ranged from collaboration to armed
resistance.

225. Zajdlerowa, Zoe. *The Dark Side of the Moon: A New
Edition*. Edited by J. Coutouvidis and Thomas Lane. London:
Harvester Wheatsheaf, 1989. 182p., ill., maps, bibl.
   The work reissued on the fiftieth anniversary of the
invasion of Poland by Nazi Germany and the Soviet Union. One
of the editors' objectives in preparing this new, second
edition was "to make it available to a new generation of
general readers at a time of intense Western interest in
political developments in Eastern Europe and the Soviet
Union" (p ix) following the Gorbachev *perestroika*.

      7a2. German Occupation

226. Cyprian, Tadeusz, and Jerzy Sawicki. *Nazi Rule in
Poland, 1939-1945*. Translated by Edward Rothert. Warsaw:
Polonia Publishing House, 1961. 261p., ill., portraits, bibl.
   A slightly abridged edition of *Nie oszczedzac Polski* issued
in 1959. Discusses Nazi aggression and occupation.

227. _____ . *Nie oszczedzac Polski /No Mercy for Poland/*.
Warszawa: Iskry, 1959. 475p., notes, portraits. Summary in
English.
   The basic documentary material on war crimes committed in
Poland from 1939-1945. Discusses Nazi aggression and
occupation, the germanization of children, Hans Frank's
diary, forced labor, public execution, and Auschwitz.
Concludes with a commentary by the authors, who were
prosecuting attorneys representing Poland at the Nuremberg
International Military Tribunal. Epilogue reviews the last
day of the trial and final statements by the accused.

228. Gross, Jan Tomasz. *Polish Society under German
Occupation: The Generalgouvernement, 1939-1944*. Princeton:
Princeton University Press, 1979. 343p., bibl.
   This study is a hybrid of sociology and history: "It
investigates old and formulates new theories of social
behavior, taking as its empirical field the German occupation
of part of Poland, the general gouvernement." (From the
preface).

229. Gumkowski, Janusz, and Kazimierz Leszczynski. *Poland
under Nazi Occupation*. Translated from Polish by Edward
Rothert. Warsaw: Polonia Publishing House, 1961. 219p.,
photogr., facsimiles, bibl.
   An account of the Nazi occupation with a variety of
rotogravure photographs, many shocking, of atrocities
perpetrated by Nazi troops. Numerous facsimiles of German
documents and orders.

      7a3. Soviet Occupation

230. Gross, Jan Tomasz. *Polska a Rosja 1939-1942 /Poland and
Russia, 1939-1942/*. London: Anex, 1983. 507p., bibl.
   A scholarly account of the deportation of Polish citizens
to Soviet labor camps during 1939-1942 after the Russian
aggression and occupation of Poland's eastern territories.

231. _____ . *Revolution from Abroad: The Soviet Conquest
of Poland's Western Ukraine and Western Belorussia*.
Princeton, NJ: Princeton University Press, 1988. 334p., ill.,
plates, bibl.
   A carefully documented study. Through extensive research
including surviving depositions and handwritten accounts by
ordinary people, Prof. Gross presents the Soviet occupation
of Poland's territories: western Ukraine and western
Belorussia, 1939-1941. He reveals the means by which the
Soviets assumed power. The topics addressed are dictated by
chronology of the elements of the Soviet presence: conquest,
elections, socialization, prisons, and deportations.

7b. CONCENTRATION AND RELATED CAMPS

7b1. German Concentration Camps (including POW camps and escape accounts)

232. Burgess, Alan. *The Longest Tunnel: The True Story of World War II's Great Escape*. New York: Grove Weidenfeld, 1990. 289p., plates, ill., portraits, bibl.
An account of the escape of 76 Allied POWs from Sagan (Zagan, Poland), Stalag Luft III, March 24, 1944, accomplished by a hand dug tunnel under the prison camp grounds. Ex-RAF flyer Burgess presents the escape as a military operation intended to disrupt the German war effort. Hitler replied by ordering that recaptured prisoners be executed by the Gestapo. The survivors' fates are described. Burgess' account is based on camp records and interviews with survivors. Recommended particularly in conjunction with A.A. Durand's *Stalag Luft III*.

233. Cohen, Elie A. *Human Behavior in the Concentration Camp*. Translated from Dutch by M. H. Braaksma. New York: Norton, 1953. 295p., ill., bibl.
A fully documented study by a Dutch physician who was himself a prisoner at Auschwitz. He analyzes the mentality of the prisoners and the SS. Basing the conclusions on his own experiences as well as on books and articles by many other inmates, the author attempts to answer the two questions: what enabled the prisoners to withstand the horrible treatment, and what caused the SS men to perpetrate such acts of barbarity?

234. Crawley, Aidan. *Escape from Germany: The Methods of Escape Used by RAF Airmen during the Second World War*. With a new introduction by H.A. Probert. London: H.M.S.O., 1985. 352p., ill.
Originally published in 1970, this is the revised edition of an absorbing, comprehensive account conveying RAF flyers' methods of escaping from German camps for Allied POWs located in the Reich's eastern territories.

235. Datner, Szymon. *Crimes against POWS: Responsibility of the Wehrmacht*. Warszawa: Zachodnia Agencja Prasowa, 1964. 382p., ill., portraits, bibl.
Story of those who, after being taken prisoner by the German Army, were exterminated or died of maltreatment, hunger, or exhaustion. Also includes accounts of other nationalities but most of the book is devoted to the Polish prisoners.

236. Durand, Arthur A. *Stalag Luft III: The Secret Story*. Baton Rouge: Louisiana State U.Press, 1988. 412p., portraits, maps, bibl.
Durand, on active duty in the US Air Force, has written an in-depth historical study of a Luftwaffe prison camp (in Zagan, Poland) that held more than 10,000 American and British flyers from 1942 to 1945. Examines many aspects of prison life including camp organization, prisoner-captor relationships, morale problems, entertainment, educational problems, covert activities (military intelligence and

escape), evacuation of the camp, and liberation.

237. Foy, David A. *For You the War Is Over: American Prisoners of War in Nazi Germany*. New York: Stein and Day, 1984. 200p., maps, charts, ill., bibl.
    Well researched, this book tells an interesting story about German policy toward American POWs in concentration camps located in Silesia (Zagan) and in occupied parts of Poland. Provides a look at camp organization, nitty-gritty details and other aspects of prison life.

238. Garlinski, Jozef. *Fighting Auschwitz: The Resistance Movement in the Concentration Camp*. London: Julian Friedman, Ltd., 1975. 327p., photos, maps, bibl.
    Related as a dispassionate, impartial and comprehensive account of the opposition by the inmates of Auschwitz and Birkenau concentration camps written thirty years after by a former inmate. Contains many portraits of resistance leaders plus photographs of the camp.

239. Gilbert, Martin. *Auschwitz and the Allies*. London: M. Joseph/ Reinbird, 1981. 368p., plates, maps, portraits, bibl.
    An account of when and how the Allies learned of Nazi atrocities against Jewish population and of their reaction. Emphasis on England and its respose to Hitler's attempted destruction of Europe's Jews.

240. International Auschwitz Committee. *Nazi Medicine: Doctors, Victims, and Medicine in Auschwitz*. 1st American ed. 3 vols. New York.: Howard Fertig, 1986. 261, 212, 227p.
    This book contains articles selected and translated for the American reader from the first special publications 1961-1967 to the Polish scientific monthly magazine *Przeglad lekarski* (*Medical Review*). The main topic covers human experimentation in medicine by Nazi doctors on the international Auschwitz concentration camp prisoners. Moral and ethical aspects of those experiments are also discussed.

241. Michalik, Krystyna, transl. and ed. *From the History of KL-Auschwitz*. 1st American ed. New York: Howard Fertig, 1982. 225p., ill.
    A collection of essays written by Polish scholars. Topical coverage includes: The concentration camp Auschwitz. The Auschwitz sub-camps. The system of punishments used by the SS in the concentration camp at Auschwitz-Birkenau. Escapes of prisoners. Ethical and legal limits in experimentation in medicine in connection with Professor Clauberg's affair. Starvation in Auschwitz. The Singer. Days of horror. Most important events in the history of the concentration camp Auschwitz-Birkenau.

242. Nyiszli, Miklos. *Auschwitz*. New York: Fell, 1960. 222p.
    Auschwitz provides an eyewitness account, particularly of SS medical doctors, by a Jewish doctor who survived by deliberately allowing himself to be used by the Nazis. The author writes of Joseph Mengele, the notorious minister of life and death and of his medical experiments--tortures really--performed on unfortunate victims.

243. Pawelczynska, Anna. *Values and Violence in Auschwitz: A Sociological Analysis*. Translated by Catherine S. Leach. Berkeley: University of California Press, 1980. 170p., ill., maps, bibl.
   This scholarly study addresses the problem of human behavior in the concentration camp. Pawelczynska shows how the prisoners formed communities and sought to give social and moral structure to their lives.

7b2. Soviet Labor Camps

244. Gross, Jan Tomasz. *Polska a Rosja 1939-1942 /Poland and Russia, 1939-1942/*. London: Anex, 1983. 507p., bibl.
   A scholarly account of the deportation of Polish citizens to Soviet labor camps during 1939-1942 after the Russian aggression and occupation of Poland's eastern territories.

245. _____ . *Revolution from Abroad: The Soviet Conquest of Poland's Western Ukraine and Western Belorussia*. Princeton, NJ: Princeton University Press, 1988. 334p., ill., plates, bibl.
   A carefully documented study. Through extensive research including surviving depositions and handwritten accounts by ordinary people, Prof. Gross presents the Soviet occupation of Poland's territories: western Ukraine and western Belorussia, 1939-1941. He reveals the means by which the Soviets assumed power. The topics addressed are dictated by chronology of the elements of the Soviet presence: conquest, elections, socialization, prisons, and deportations.

246. Krolikowski, Lucjan. *Stolen Childhood: A Saga of Polish War Children*. Translated from Polish by Kazimierz J. Rozniakowski. Buffalo, N.Y.: Father Justin Rosary Hour, 1983. 296p., ill., portraits, maps, bibl.
   A description of the plight of thousands of Polish children deported to Soviet Russia and thereafter left homeless, some 380,000, between 1939 and 1941. Consists of four parts: "Deportation to Russia", "In Africa", "Through Europe", and "In Canada".

247. Piesakowski, Tomasz. *The Fate of Poles in the USSR, 1939-1989*. Translated by Anna Marianska. Preface by Dr. Robert Conquest and Edward Raczynski. London: Gryf Publications, 1990. 359p., plates, photos, maps, bibl.
   Based on extensive documentation, mostly Polish, the book provides a detailed account of the fate of Poles deported to Soviet labor camps during the last fifty years following the Russian aggression in 1939. Ambassador Raczynski regards Piesakowski's study as "a veritable encyclopedia of violations of human rights ... and all manner of cruelty and treachery." Supported by rich documentary evidence, including photographs, maps, statistical data, and bibliographical references, the book is an important contribution to the growing literature of the subject.

248. Sword, Keith. *Deportation and Exile: Poles in the Soviet Union, 1939-48*. New York: St. Martin's Press in association with School of Slavonic and East European Studies, University

of London, 1994. 269p., maps, bibl. (Studies in Russia and
East Europe series).
   An amply documented study concentrating on the mass
movement of the Polish population: forced, state-inspired or
organized displacing and repatriation, refugee flight from
armed conflict, migration to join the newly-formed Polish
armed forces (and to leave captivity), mass scale exodus
across state borders. The author seeks to set all the subject
in a broader political and diplomatic context.

249. Wittlin, Tadeusz. *Time Stopped at 6:30*. Indianapolis,
Ind.: Bobbs-Merril Co., 1965. 317p., ill., portraits, maps,
bibl.
   First and factual account of the thousands of Polish
prisoners in concentration camps in Soviet Russia. This is an
historical account. Numerous references to the Katyn Forest
Massacre of 1940 including sections from U.S. House of
Representatives, 82nd Congress, Final Report of the Select
Committee "to conduct an investigation and study of the
facts, evidence, and circumstances of the Katyn Forest
Massacre".

7c. ATROCITIES, GERMAN AND SOVIET

7c1. General Accounts

250. Bartoszewski, Wladyslaw. *Warsaw Death Ring, 1939-1944*.
Translated from Polish by Edward Rothert. Warszawa:
Interpress, 1968. 450p., ill., portraits, maps, bibl.
   First thoroughly documented attempt in Polish historical
literature to record the losses suffered by the people of
Warsaw in 1939-1945. Concerned chiefly with the main
executions of the Polish residents of the city. The tragedy
of the Jewish population has been outlined in a special
chapter. Contains numerous lists of persons executed.

251. Bolewski, Andrzej, and Henryk Pierzchala. *Losy polskich
pracownikow nauki w latach 1939-1945: straty osobowe /Fates
of the Polish Scholars, 1939-1945: War Casualties/*. Wroclaw:
Zaklad Narodowy im. Ossolinskich, 1989. 750p., plates, ill.,
bibl. Summary in English, German, and Russian.
   This massive volume is a record of heavy losses suffered by
Polish science--the loss of faculty members of scientific
institutions in the wartime years. Names, photographs, maps,
statistical data are the documentary basis of the study.

252. Datner, Szymon. *Genocide 1939-1945*. Warszawa: Wyd.
Zachodnie, 1962. 334p., ill., facsims. bibl.
   Nazi atrocities in Poland. The work is based on documents
assembled by the Central Commission for the Investigation of
Nazi Crimes in Poland, published in the years 1945-1960.

253. Davies, Norman, and Antony Polonsky, eds. *Jews in
Eastern Poland and the USSR, 1939-46*. London: St. Martin's,
1991. 426p., maps, bibl. (Studies in Russia and East Europe
Series).
   Essays dealt with in this collection include: the role of
Jews in the sovietization of Eastern Poland between 1939 and

1941; the effect of this period on Jewish response to the
subsequent Nazi conquest and initiation of the "final
solution"; the role Jews played in the years when the USSR
reconquered the area and began to establish a communist-
dominated regime in Poland; and the fate of Polish citizens
of Jewish descent in the USSR. Contributors to this volume
are scholars from Poland, Israel, the USSR, England, and the
United States.

254. Hrabar, Roman Zbigniew, Zofia Tokarz, and Jacek E.
Wilczur. *The Fate of Polish Children during the Last War.*
Translated from Polish by Bogdan Buczkowski and Lech
Petrowicz. With introd. by Janusz Wieczorek. Warsaw:
Interpress, 1981. 213p., ill., portraits, maps, tables, bibl.
Translation of *Czas niewoli, czas smierci.*
   Children and youth shared the fate of their elders, with
them they fought and perished. They were killed during the
pacification operations in Zamosc, Kielce and Lublin regions,
perished in gas chambers and crematoria in Nazi extermination
camps. This documentary study is devoted to those youngest
victims of the Second World War. The topic is described in
the chapters: 1. "The Nazi concepts and programmes for the
extermination of children"; 2. "Extermination of Polish
children"; 3. "Abduction and germanization"; 4. "The fate of
Jewish children"; 5. "Children saved from extermination"; 6.
"The effects of war and Nazi occupation on children's psychic
life"; 7. "Nazi apparatus of crime". Richly photo-documented.

255. Lukas, Richard C. *Did the Chidren Cry?: Hitler's War
against Jewish and Polish Children, 1939-1945.* New York:
Hippocrene Books, 1994. 263p., plates, ill., bibl.
   The noted writer on Polish wartime matters, Lukas in his
last book "deals with the lifetimes of Jewish and gentile
children of Poland, where the Nazis had established the most
efficient killing center in Europe." A mass of documentary
material.

256. Madajczyk, Czeslaw. *Hitlerowski terror na wsi polskiej,
1939-1945 /Nazi Terror in Polish Villages, 1939-1945/.*
Contrib. by Stanislawa Lewandowska. Warszawa: Panstw. Wyd.
Nauk., 1965. 169p., tables, bibl. Introduction in English.
   Arranged by districts and chronology of acts, this
publication is a record of major Nazi atrocities in Polish
villages. Based mainly on Polish sources because the
repressive actions against village populations were usually
not made public by posters.

257. Malcher, George Charles. *Blank Pages: Soviet Genocide
against the Polish People.* Foreword by Rt. Hon. Lord Braine
Wheatley. Pyrford: Pyrford Press, 1993. 201p., ill., maps,
bibl.
   It has taken decades for the full horror of Stalin's
calculated cruelties--terror, concentration camps,
starvation, Katyn and other massacres--to become known. There
have been so many "Blank Pages" until recent years in the
history of Polish-Soviet relations "that we owe it to those
who perished, to their descendants, and to free peoples
everywhere to make the facts known" (the Foreword). The
author intends to reveal only selected instances of what

happened. The book is a compendium on the subject.

258. Marczewski, Jerzy. *Hitlerowska koncepcja polityki
kolonizacyjno-wysiedlenczej i jej realizacja w "Okregu Warty"
/The Nazi Conception of Colonization and Deportation and Its
Implementation in the Warta Region (Warthegau)/*. Poznan:
Instytut Zachodni, 1979. 488p., maps, ill., bibl. Summary in
English.
Provides an analysis of the colonization and deportation
policy in the Warta Region. Conclusion: that strategy was the
fullest expression of the Nazi plans for German expansion in
the East. The implementation of the plans included all
available means: police methods, terror, and even genocide.
Extensive bibliography.

259. Pilichowski, Czeslaw. *No Time-Limit for These Crimes*.
Translated from Polish by Jan Sek. Warsaw: Interpress, 1980.
186p., ill., facsims, bibl.
Describes the treatment of the Polish people, including
Jews, by the Nazi occupant. Covers deportation, labor and
concentration camps, and other forms of atrocities.

260. Stypulkowski, Zbigniew. *Invitation to Moscow*. Preface by
H. R. Trevor-Roper. London: Thames and Hudson, 1951. 359p.
The author, a Polish lawyer and a survivor of the Soviet
Lubianka prison, gives nearly a clinical report on political
terror and other methods used by the Soviets to obtain a
confession of his non-guilt. The book is also important
because Stypulkowski, a Home Army soldier, provides the
detailed story of the Soviet perfidy toward the Polish
underground in the closing days of the Warsaw uprising.

7c2. War Crimes and War Criminals

261. Bartoszewski, Wladyslaw. *Erich von dem Bach*. Warsaw:
Wydawn. Zachodnie, 1961. 109p., ill., facsims., bibl.
A detailed and absorbing picture of the personality and
activities of war criminal Erich von dem Bach. Bartoszewski
characterizes his political ability and perfidy of the
methods used. Based mostly on German documents.

262. Cyprian, Tadeusz, and Jerzy Sawicki. *Nie oszczedzac
Polski /No Mercy for Poland/*. Warszawa: Iskry, 1959. 475p.,
notes, portraits. Summary in English.
The basic documentary material on war crimes committed in
Poland from 1939-1945. Discusses Nazi aggression and
occupation, the germanization of children, Hans Frank's
diary, forced labor, public execution, and Auschwitz.
Concludes with a commentary by the authors, who were
prosecuting attorneys representing Poland at the Nuremberg
International Military Tribunal. Epilogue reviews the last
day of the trial and final statements by the accused.

263. Glowna Komisja Badania Zbrodni Niemieckich w Polsce.
Zbrodnie niemieckie w Polsce /German Crimes in Poland/. Vols
1-3. English. Selections. Central Commission for
Investigation of German Crimes in Poland. 1st American ed.
New York: Howard Fertig, 1982. 271, 168p., plates, ill.,

facsims, maps, plans, bibl.

Originally published in Warsaw in 1946-47, this is a translation, with some omissions and condensations, of documents contained in 3 volumes of the *Biuletyn Glownej Komisji Badania Zbrodni Niemieckich w Polsce* on German crimes in Poland: concentration camps, atrocities, the Holocaust.

264. Lukowski, Stanislaw. *Zbrodnie hitlerowskie na Slasku Opolskim w latach 1933-1945 /Nazi Crimes in Opole Silesia, 1933-1945/*. Wroclaw: Zakl. Nar. im. Ossolinskich, 1979. 200p., ill., bibl. (Monografie slaskie series, 30). Summary in English, German, and Russian.

This extensively researched study presents ample evidence for Nazi crimes in Opole Silesia from Hitler's rise to power through 1945. Economic and strategic role of Opole Silesia in the Reich's war planning is explored and seen as the principal cause of German ruthless actions, especially over the period of 1939, aimed at destruction of all "Polish elements". The study relies on German, Soviet, and Polish sources.

265. Muszkat, Marian. *Polish Charges against German War Criminals*. Warsaw: The National Office for the Investigation of German War Crimes, 1948. 232p.

Contains excerpts from 18 cases submitted to the United Nations War Crimes Committee.

266. Pilichowski, Czeslaw, ed. *Zbrodnie i sprawcy: ludobojstwo hitlerowskie przed sadem ludzkosci i historii /Nazi Crimes in the Court of Humanity and History/*. Warszawa: PWN, 1980. 943p., ill., bibl. Summaries and table of contents in English, French, and Russian.

A compilation of materials prepared by various authors for commemorating the 30th anniversary of the General Commission for Investigation of Nazi Crimes in Poland. The "publication is a review of the state of knowledge in the field of war crimes, crimes against humanity, and a review of results of prosecuting their perpetrators." A detailed problem-oriented table of contents and summaries in several languages.

267. Pilichowski, Zdzislaw, ed. *Dzieci i mlodziez w latach drugiej wojny swiatowej /Children and Youth in World War II/*. Warszawa: PWN, 1982. 611p., bibl. Summary in English, German and Russian.

This publication is a collection of papers prepared for the topical International Scientific Session held in Warsaw, 1979. Problems addressed include crimes committed by the Nazis against children and youth, and the nations' struggles to protect children from biological extermination, denationalization and depravation, and the young people's contribution to the struggle against the Nazis during the war.

268. Piotrowski, Stanislaw, ed. *Hans Frank's Diary*. Warszawa: PWN, 1961. 320p., ill., bibl.

A systematic record of the most important aspects of war crimes committed by Hans Frank while Governor General in Cracow. Based on scientific, objective, and impartial analysis of the vast amount of material included in Frank's

diary and in documents brought to light at the course of the
Nuremberg Trial.

269. Winiewicz, Jozef M. *Aims and Failures of the German New
Order: A Study*. Chicago: American Polish Council, 1943.
119p., bibl.
Examines Hitler's systematic attempts of germanizing the
western parts of Poland by exterminating Polish minorities
("Polish elements") and bringing in the "pure" German
settlers.

7c3. The Holocaust (including the Warsaw and other ghettos, Uprising, and aid to Jews)

270. Ainsztein, Reuben. *The Warsaw Ghetto Revolt*. New York:
Schocken Books, 1979. 238p., ill., portraits, bibl.
A story of the Warsaw Ghetto uprising by one of the
outstanding experts on the Jewish resistance in Eastern
Europe. Portraits of many participants.

271. Bartoszewski, Wladyslaw. *The Blood Shed Unites Us: Pages
from the History of Help to the Jews in Occupied Poland*.
Warsaw: Interpress, 1970. 243p., ill., facsims, portraits.
Focusing mainly on the events that took place in Warsaw,
the author gives an outline history of the assistance by the
Polish underground to Jews in the wartime years. These
efforts are placed in the context of the general situation in
the occupied country.

272. _____ . *The Warsaw Ghetto: A Christian's Testimony*.
Foreword by Stanislaw Lem. Translated from German by Stephen
G. Cappellari. Boston: Beacon Press, 1987. 117 p., plates,
ill.
This book about the Warsaw Ghetto and the eventual
deportation and extermination of the Jews living there is
written by a Polish historian and Poland's Minister of
Foreign Affairs in 1994-95. Bartoszewski worked during the
war for the Polish Council for Aid to Jews and other
organizations, which attempted to assist the 70,000 to
100,000 Jews remaining in Warsaw after the main liquidation
of the ghetto there in 1942. The book outlines the efforts to
supply surviving Jews with forged documents, food, and
shelter, and to arouse public opinion in the West.
Bartoszewski is the author of 18 books and nearly 500
articles on the Holocaust.

273. Bartoszewski, Wladyslaw, and Zofia Lewinowna. *The
Samaritans: Heroes of the Holocaust*. Translated from Polish.
American ed. by Alexander T. Jordan. New York: Twayne, 1970.
442p.
The story of the "Polish Council for Aid to Jews" and its
efforts to help save Polish Jewry from the Holocaust. The
author was one of the Council's founders and leaders from
1942 to 1944. This work is based on personal memories,
first-hand accounts, newspapers and archival materials.

274. Berenstein, Tatiana, and Adam Rutkowski. *Assistance to the Jews in Poland, 1939-1945.* Translated by Edward Rothert. Warsaw: Polonia Publishing House, 1963. 82p., ill., portraits, bibl. Translation of *Pomoc Zydom w Polsce, 1939-1945.*
"The book is intended to show the sacrifice of those who, despite the raging terror and their own tragedies and war misfortunes, risked their lives to bring relief to the most stricken members of the community, the Jews". (From the introd.) Fully documented.

275. Davies, Norman, and Antony Polonsky, eds. *Jews in Eastern Poland and the USSR, 1939-46.* London: St. Martin's, 1991. 426p., maps, bibl. (Studies in Russia and East Europe series).
Essays dealt with in this collection include: the role of Jews in the sovietization of Eastern Poland between 1939 and 1941; the effect of this period on Jewish response to the subsequent Nazi conquest and initiation of the "final solution"; the role Jews played in the years when the USSR reconquered the area and began to establish a communist-dominated regime in Poland; and the fate of Polish citizens of Jewish descent in the USSR. Contributors to this volume are scholars from Poland, Israel, the USSR, England, and the United States.

276. Friedman, Philip, ed. *Martyrs and Fighters: The Epic of the Warsaw Ghetto.* New York: Praeger, 1954. 325p.
This selection of eyewitness accounts of the Warsaw Ghetto gives the reader a realistic picture of the Nazi efforts to annihilate the Jews. There is an attempt to be objective and both Jewish heroism and discreditable acts are shown. The book also describes the resistance to the Nazis by the Ghetto's Jewish Fighting Organization.

277. Gilbert, Martin. *Auschwitz and the Allies.* London: M. Joseph Reinbird, 1981. 368p., plates, maps, portraits, bibl.
An account of when and how the Allies learned of Nazi atrocities against Jewish population and of their reaction. Emphasis on England and its respose to Hitler's attempted destruction of Europe's Jews.

278. Glowna Komisja Badania Zbrodni Niemieckich w Polsce. *Zbrodnie niemieckie w Polsce /German Crimes in Poland/.* Vols 1-3. English. Selections. /Central Commission for Investigation on German Crimes in Poland/. 1st American ed. New York: Howard Fertig, 1982. 271, 168p., plates, ill., facsims, maps, plans, bibl.
Originally published in Warsaw in 1946-47, this is a translation, with some omissions and condensations, of documents contained in 3 volumes of the *Biuletyn Glownej Komisji Badania Zbrodni Niemieckich w Polsce* on German crimes in Poland: concentration camps, atrocities, the Holocaust.

279. Gutman, Israel. *Resistance: The Warsaw Ghetto Uprising.* Boston: Houghton Mifflin, 1994. 277p., ill., maps, bibl.
Resistance provides a comprehensive coverage of the Warsaw Ghetto uprising of April 1943, its background and course. This historic event, which has become a symbol of Jewish

resistance and determination, is told by a man who survived
the battle and is now a noted Israeli scholar and expert on
the Holocaust.

280. Iranek-Osmecki, Kazimierz. *He Who Saves One Life*. New
York: Crown Publishers, 1971. 336p., bibl.
   As soon as the Nazis entered Poland, they began a wholesale
persecution of the Jewish population. There were many Poles
who actively opposed the German butchery and risked their
lives and the lives of their families to help the Jews. In
this book Osmecki provides remarkable documentation of Polish
aid to the hunted.

281. Korbonski, Stefan. *The Jews and the Poles in World War
II*. New York: Hippocrene Books, 1988. 240p., ill., bibl.
   When the systematic extermination of the Jews by the
Germans began, the Polish Underground started to send
messages to the Allied leaders. While the Allies did nothing,
the Poles saved almost 100,000 Jewish lives. Subject to
automatic death sentences for helping the Jews, thousands of
Poles paid with their lives for aiding or sheltering the
Jews. Korbonski, the winner of the Yad Vashem medal for
saving the Jews, has a lot to say about it in his book.

282. Landau, Elaine. *The Warsaw Ghetto Uprising*. New York:
Maxwell Macmillan International, 1992. 143p., ill., bibl.
   The book describes life in the section of Warsaw where
Polish Jews were confined by the Nazis in the early 1940s.
Emphasis is placed on the final days of fighting prior to the
destruction of the Ghetto in 1943.

283. Lewin, Abraham. *A Cup of Tears: A Diary of the Warsaw
Ghetto*. Edited by Antony Polonsky; translation of the diary
by Christopher Hutton. Oxford: Blackwell, 1988, 310p.,
plates, maps. Published "in association with the Institute
for Polish-Jewish Studies, Oxford".
   Before his death, Lewin, a 47-year-old school teacher kept
this diary covering the period from April 1942 through
January 1943, in order to record the events in the ghetto.
The manuscript survived in an archive secreted in milk-
churns. Polonsky's lengthy introduction and over 500
footnotes provide a deep historical background of life in the
ghetto, whereas Lewin himself gives us a clear and objective
picture of daily activities in the ghetto. Topics covered
include: rationing, fears, his own and his friends' personal
tragedies, deportations, tensions among Jews, and
collaboration with the Nazis.

284. Lukas, Richard C., ed. *Out of the Inferno: Poles
Remember the Holocaust*. Lexington: University Press of
Kentucky, 1989. 201p., plates, ill., bibl.
   This book is a selection of oral and written memoirs of
some 60 Polish men and women who lived through the German
occupation of Poland in WW II. The contributors derive from a
wide social and political background. Most recollections are
descriptive rather than evaluative. They discuss some aspect
of the Jewish Holocaust and some describe their efforts on
behalf of Jews. Only a few refer candidly to animosities
between Poles and Jews.

285. Mark, Bernard, ed. *The Stroop Report: The Jewish Quarter in Warsaw Is No More!*. Translated from German by Sybil Milton. London: Secker & Warburg, 1980. 132p., portraits, photostatic materials.
   Covers in detail the famous report by Juergen Stroop concerning the Uprising in the Ghetto of Warsaw and the liquidation of the Jewish residential area. Identifies most of the Germans who carried out the destruction. Based on primary documents.

285a. Newton, Verne W., ed. *FDR and the Holocaust*. New York: St. Martin's Press, 1995.
N.A.

286. Tec, Nechama. *When Light Pierced the Darkness: Christian Rescue of Jews in Nazi-Occupied Poland*. New York: Oxford University Press, 1985. 262p., bibl.
   The author, an associate professor of sociology at the University of Connecticut, offers an extensively researched "study of Christian rescue of Jews in Nazi-occupied Poland, based on 65 in-depth personal interviews with the rescuers and survivors".

287. Tenenbaum, Joseph Leib. *Underground: The Story of a People*. New York: Philosophical Library, 1952. 532p., ill., bibl.
   Annotated, with a bibliography and index, this is a detailed description of the mass extermination of Jews in Poland under Nazi tyranny. Much material deals with the Jewish underground and battle for the Warsaw Ghetto.

288. Tenenbaum, Joseph Leib, and Sheila Tenenbaum. *In Search of a Lost People: The Old and the New Poland*. New York: Beechhurst Press, 1948. 312p., bibl.
   The authors tell the tragedy that befell the Jews during the war and give the ghastly details of the German camps of extermination in the Warsaw, Lodz, Cracow and other ghettos. The book is a worthy historical survey for the general reader as well as a guide to scholars.

289. Werstein, Irving. *The Uprising of the Warsaw Ghetto, November 1940-May 1943*. New York: Norton, 1968. 157p., ill., portraits, maps, bibl.
   Describes the resistance of the Jews of Warsaw. Drawn from trial records, published sources and interviews, the account shows both the collaborators and heroes, the inhuman and humane.

290. Wood, E. Thomas, and Stanislaw M. Jankowski. *Karski: How One Man Tried to Stop the Holocaust*. Foreword by Elie Wiesel. New York: John Wiley, 1994. 316p., plates, ill., map, bibl.
   The authors' goal was to present a chronological and factual account of Jan Karski's wartime activities. The book recounts the Polish Army officer's heroic and exciting escapades: Nazi and Soviet imprisonment, escapes, his service as a secret agent for the Polish underground. Focus is on Karski's struggles as a diplomatic courier to aid the Home Army, and to inform the world's VIPs about the Nazi atrocities in the Warsaw Ghetto and elsewhere. His testimony

was not taken seriously. "Some refused to listen to him, others to believe him", points out E. Wiesel in the foreword. Based on Karski's oral reminiscences and extensive reading of Polish and foreign materials, this biography of the young Polish Catholic is valuable for it tempers the wide-spread contention that Gentle Poland was indifferent to the plight of the Jews. (See also Karski-author in this bibliography).

7c4. The Katyn Forest Massacre

291. Abarinov, Vladimir. *The Murderers of Katyn. First American edition.* Foreword and chronology by Iwo Pogonowski. New York: Hippocrene Books, 1993. 396p., bibl.
  The facts of Katyn, long known outside the Soviet Union, could be published by the author in Russia in 1991 only after Gorbachev and Yeltsin had both acknowledged the Soviets' responsibility for the ghastly deed. Abarinov was allowed to examine only a fraction of Russian archival materials. Nevertheless, this is an important addition to the Katyn studies.

292. FitzGibbon, Louis. *Katyn: A Crime without Parallel.* Introd. by Constantine FitzGibbon. New York: Scribner, 1971. 285p., ill., facsims, map, portraits, bibl.
  Although the book was intended to provide the fullest account to date of the Katyn massacre, it fails to achieve its objective. Ten years after Zawodny's publication (*Death in the Forest,* 1962), FitzGibbon does not add much to our knowledge of the crime.

293. Mackiewicz, Jozef. *The Crime of Katyn. Facts and Documents.* With a foreword by Wladyslaw Anders. 3rd ed. London: Polish Cultural Foundation, 1965. 303p., plates, maps, ill., bibl.
  When the International Military Tribunal in Nuremberg pronounced its sentence in the fall of 1946, the Katyn crime was not mentioned among the atrocities. This book is an account of the massacre of Polish officers in the Katyn Forest, in April 1940. Traces the development of the investigation, including the refusal of the Soviet government to allow the Investigative Committee of the Red Cross to be sent to the scene, the publication of German documents, and the Soviet Commission's communique of January 1944. Based on primary materials. The book is also important by virtue of the person of General Wladyslaw Anders, the prisoner himself of the Soviets (1941), and later commander in chief of the Polish forces formed in the Soviet Union to fight against Germany. He led his troops to the West.

294. Paul, Allen. *Katyn: The Untold Story of Stalin's Polish Massacre.* New York: C. Scribner's Sons, 1991, 390 p., maps, bibl.
  A journalist, Paul combines in his book a great narrative power with a massive collection of written documents and numerous personal interviews. As a result, the reader is given a moving, detailed reconstruction of the Katyn story, placed in a broader context of diplomatic issues. The book is enhanced by some of recently available Russian archival

records. Along with Zawodny's *Death in the forest*, Paul's
study is the most comprehensive and up-to-date coverage of
the subject.

295. U.S. Congress. House. Select Committee on the Katyn
Forest Massacre. *The Katyn Forest Massacre*. Washington, DC:
Government Printing Office, 1952. 7 parts in 2 vols (2362p.),
maps.
    A massive compilation of testimony and documents relating
to the massacre of thousands of Polish officers in the Katyn
Forest near Smolensk, Russia. The hearings were held in
Washington and Germany. Witnesses and documents include
American, Polish, and Russian sources. The charge to the
House Committee was "to conduct a full and complete
investigation and study of the facts, evidence and
extenuating circumstances both before and after the massacre
of thousands of Polish officers..." The Committee concluded
that the Russians, not the Germans, were responsible for the
massacre.

296. Wittlin, Tadeusz. *Time Stopped at 6:30*. Indianapolis,
Ind.: Bobbs-Merril Co., 1965. 317p., ill., portraits, maps,
bibl.
    First and factual account of thousands of Polish prisoners
in concentration camps in the Soviet Russia. This is an
historical account. Numerous references to Katyn Forest
Massacre of 1940 including sections from U.S. House of
Representatives, 82nd Congress, Final Report of the Select
Committee "to conduct an investigation and study of the
facts, evidence, and circumstances of the Katyn Forest
Massacre".

297. Zawodny, Janusz Kazimierz. *Death in the Forest: The
Story of the Katyn Forest Massacre*. Notre Dame: University of
Notre Dame Press, 1962. 235p., ill, bibl. (International
Studies of the Committee on International Relations series,
University of Notre Dame).
    A standard scholarly account of the Katyn Forest Massacre,
near Smolensk, Ukraine, in 1940. The author, who fought in
the Polish underground, presents an unemotional account of
the "disappearance" or massacre of some 15,000 Poles and
Polish Jews, including some 8,000 officers. The book tries to
answer three questions: "Who killed these men? How were they
killed? Why were they killed?"

7d. DEMOGRAPHIC CHANGES AND SHIFTS, DISPLACED PERSONS,
      CHILDREN (for population transfer, see also 8a2. The
      German Problem: The Western Territories and
      Resettlement)

298. Burstin, Barbara Stern. *After the Holocaust: The
Migration of Polish Jews and Christians to Pittsburgh*.
Pittsburgh: Pittsburgh University Press, 1989. 219p., bibl.
    Based on interviews with the survivors and on records of
the local and national organizations that assisted in the
resettlement of displaced persons, Burstin's book offers a
fresh perspective on the Holocaust through a comparative
study of 60 Jews and 60 Christians. The narrative follows

these emigrants from the prewar years in Poland, through
their wartime experiences, their decision to emigrate, and
their early adjustment to life in the United States, to their
attitudes and circumstances today. For all readers.

299. De Zayas, Alfred M. *Nemesis at Potsdam: The Anglo-
Americans and the Expulsion of the Germans: Background,
Execution, Consequences*. 2nd ed. London; Boston: Routledge &
Kegan Paul, 1977. 268p., plates, ill., bibl.
    Examines in detail the concept of mass population
transfers, how they came to be accepted at Potsdam and how
the Allies tried to keep them "orderly and humane", in vain.

300. Gruchman, Bohdan. *Polish Western Territories*. Translated
from Polish by Wanda Libicka. Poznan: Instytut Zachodni,
1959. 267p., maps, bibl.
    The purpose of this book is to collect and elaborate on the
basic information concerning the Polish western territories.
Avoids polemics and propaganda, trying instead to "allow
figures and facts that have been confirmed and discussed many
times to speak for themselves". They are used to describe
demographic changes and dynamic economic development of the
recovered regions.

301. Kamenetsky, Ihor. *Secret Nazi Plans for Eastern Europe:
A Study of Lebensraum Policies*. New York: Bookman Associates,
1961. 263p., bibl.
    This in-depth scholarly study first acquaints the reader
with ideological and political background of Nazi *Lebensraum*
policy and then examines in detail the German conceptions and
secret plans for colonization of East European populations:
Poles, Jews, Czechs, Lithuanians. Hitler used any method to
implement those plans: resettlement, deportation, repression,
concentration camps, and extermination. Based on a wide body
of source materials.

302. Kersten, Krystyna. *Repatriacja ludnosci polskiej po II
wojnie swiatowej: studium historyczne /Repatriation of the
Polish Population after the Second World War: A Historical
Study/*. Wroclaw: Ossolineum. Polish Academy of Sciences
Institute of History, 1974. 277p., bibl. Summary in English.
    The study analyzes the emigration of the Polish population
as a result of war campaigns and the defeat of Poland.
Characterizes movements of people from territories
incorporated into the USSR in 1939, deportations to
compulsory work in the Third Reich, deportations resulting
from Nazi repressions towards civilian population,
demographic consequences of service in the Wehrmacht, and the
shifting of many thousands of ex-soldiers to western
countries after the war.

303. Koehl, Robert L. *RKFDV: German Resettlement and
Population Policy 1939-1945: A History of the Reich
Commission for the Strengthening of Germandom*. Cambridge,
Mass.: Harvard University Press, 1957. 263p., bibl. (Harvard
Historical Monographs, 31).
    A well documented, thorough analysis of characteristic
aspects of Nazi population policy during World War II. The
author describes attempts at resettlement especially in

Polish areas under German control. The study is primarily
based on unpublished material collected for and used by
prosecution and defense at Nuremberg in United States Trials
8 and 11. For researchers.

304. Kokot, Jozef. *The Logic of the Oder-Neisse Frontier*.
Poznan: Wydawn. Zach., 1959. 289p., bibl.
   Approaches the problem of the postwar changes of western
boundaries, as established on the Oder-Neisse line, from the
standpoint of international law and deals with the
demographic and economic implications of the new frontiers.

305. Krolikowski, Lucjan. *Stolen Childhood: A Saga of Polish
War Children*. Translated from Polish by Kazimierz J.
Rozniakowski. Buffalo, N.Y.: Father Justin Rosary Hour, 1983.
296p., ill., portraits, maps, bibl.
   A description of the plight of thousands of Polish children
deported to Soviet Russia and thereafter left homeless, some
380,000, between 1939 and 1941. Consists of four parts:
"Deportation to Russia", "In Africa", "Through Europe", and
"In Canada".

306. Kruszewski, Z. Anthony. *The Oder-Neisse Boundary and
Poland's Modernization: The Socioeconomic and Political
Impact*. Foreword by Morton A. Kaplan. New York: Praeger,
1972. 245p., maps, bibl.
   The main point of Dr. Kruszewski's study is that the
acquisition of the territories east of the Oder-Neisse was
the determining factor for Poland's modernization and
economic advance after World War II, due to the shift of
resource and manpower base. Deals with population migrations
and the fluctuating economic structure of the region.
Numerous statistical data, bibliographic sources (mostly
Polish), the appendix including the treaty between Poland and
German Democratic Republic, as well as between Poland and
Federal Republic of Germany add to the value of this volume.

307. Schechtman, Joseph. *European Population Transfers,
1939-1945*. New York: Oxford University Press, 1946. 532p.,
maps, bibl. (Studies of the Institute of World Affairs).
   Describes Hitler's deportations of German minorities from
South Tyrol, and East European population exchanges--Poles,
Ukrainians, Czechs, etc., during the occupation. This
factual, well-documented study was prepared for the Institute
of World Affairs.

308. Sword, Keith, Norman Davies, and Jan Ciechanowski. *The
Formation of the Polish Community in Great Britain 1939-1950:
The M.B. Grabowski Polish Migration Project Report*. London::
School of Slavonic and East European Studies, University of
London, 1989. 498p., plates, ill., maps, portraits, bibl.
   A book of great rarity. Based on a thorough reading of
British and Polish government archival materials, and other
primary sources, this work provides a chronological,
political, and socio-economic analysis of the origins of the
Polish community in early postwar Britain. Section III is of
special interest: it examines the administrative and
sociological problems involved in the process of
resettlement.

309. Wyman, Mark. *DP: Europe's Displaced Persons, 1945-1951*.
Philadelphia; London: Balch Institute Press; Associated
University Presses, 1989. 257p., ill., bibl.
   This is a study of the social, economic, and political
circumstances within which relocation, resettlement, and
repatriation of millions of people, including many Poles,
occurred as a result of the war. The value of this account is
especially enhanced by the author's numerous interviews with
former DPs, and the selective use of basic contemporary
archival and secondary works.

310. Zielinski, Henryk. *Population Changes in Poland,
1939-1950*. New York: Mid-European Studies Center, 1954.
101p., bibl.
   Reviews selected aspects of the changes in demographic
structure of Poland caused by the war, the joint occupation
of her territory by Germany and the Soviet Russia, and
subsequent shifts in boundaries.

7e. INFORMATION MEDIA (press, radio, propaganda)

311. Batowski, Henryk. *Walka dyplomacji hitlerowskiej przeciw
Polsce, 1939-1945 /Nazi Diplomacy against Poland, 1939-1945/*.
Krakow: Wyd. Literackie, 1984. 207p., bibl. Summary in
English and German.
   Describes propaganda methods used by the Nazis in their
diplomatic warfare against, at first, the Polish state and
later against the Government-in-exile. The aim of these
attacks was to discredit Poland, particularly in the eyes of
neutral countries.

312. Burleigh, Michael. *Germany Turns Eastwards: A Study of
Ostforschung in the Third Reich*. Cambridge: Cambridge
University Press, 1988. 351p., ill., maps, portraits, bibl.
   Burleigh (London School of Economics and Political Science)
presents a fascinating aspect of the involvement of German
academics who were Ostforscher (researchers on Eastern
Europe), in the Nazi's rule over this region. The focus is on
Poland. Scholars were enlisted to produce studies,
recommendations and propaganda that were to help the Nazi
authorities to segregate, divide, and rule conquered
populations, or to replace them with German ethnic stock.

313. Dobroszycki, Lucjan. *Reptile Journalism: The Official
Polish-Language Press under the Nazis, 1939-1945*. Translated
by Barbara Harshav. New Haven: Yale University Press, 1994.
199p., ill., bibl.
   A well documented account of the underground press in
Poland. Drawn mainly from Polish archival records, the study
is a useful source of information on wartime Poland.

314. Lewandowska, Stanislawa. *Polska konspiracyjna prasa
informacyjno-polityczna, 1939-1945. /Polish Underground
Press, 1939-1945/*. Warszawa: Czytelnik, 1982. 445p., plates,
ill., bibl.
   This scholarly monograph provides a systematic analysis,
evaluation and conclusions regarding aims and goals,
organization and operation of the Polish underground press

and literature. Extensive footnotes and comparisons with peer
resistance press in the occupied Europe are made. A valuable
contribution to the history of liberation propaganda media of
the war period.

7f. CULTURAL, RELIGIOUS, AND MORAL ASPECTS OF THE WAR

315. Balawyder, A. *The Odyssey of the Polish Treasures*.
Antigonish, Nova Scotia: St. Francis Xavier University Press,
1978. 107p., ill., plates, bibl.
    Relates "the saga of the [national] art treasures as they
left the Wawel Royal Castle in Cracow after September 1939,
their dangerous odyssey to France, England, and finally to
Canada, their sojourn" for two decades. Also details the
political problems involved with their release and return to
the homeland. Enhanced by numerous illustrations.

316. De Jaeger, Charles. *The Linz File: Hitler's Plunder of
Europe's Art*. Toronto: John Wiley & Sons, 1981. 192p., ill.,
bibl.
    The story of Hitler's design to build the world's largest
museum of German and European art in Linz, Austria. The
author consulted the existing literature of the subject and
interviewed surviving German and Austrian participants of
these events to discover that Hitler's desire to gain
absolute control of European art must be traced to his
boyhood in Linz. Several chapters describe the acquisition of
art works from such conquered lands as Austria, Poland,
Czechoslovakia, the Low Countries, and France (and even from
Fascist Italy) by plunder, purchase, confiscation, and
negotiations. Two chapters discuss the recovery of Europe's
art works. An entertaining book on an interesting subject.

317. Graham, Robert A. *The Pope and Poland in World War Two*.
With a preface by John Cardinal Krol. London: Veritas, 1968.
62p., portraits.
    A scholarly summary of documents in Vatican archives
entitled *The religious situation in Poland and the Baltic
states, 1939-1945*. Throws light on the situation of the
Catholic Church in Poland during the German occupation and
the pontificate of Pope Pius XII.

318. International Auschwitz Committee. *Nazi Medicine:
Doctors, Victims, and Medicine in Auschwitz*. 1st American ed.
3 vols. New York : Howard Fertig, 1986. 261, 212, 227p.
    This book contains articles selected and translated for the
American reader from the first special publications 1961-1967
to the Polish scientific monthly magazine *Przeglad lekarski
(Medical Review)*. The main topic covers human experimentation
in medicine by Nazi doctors on the international Auschwitz
concentration camp prisoners. Moral and ethical aspects of
those experiments are also discussed.

319. Madajczyk, Czeslaw. *Inter Arma Non Silent Musae: The War
and the Culture, 1939-1945*. Warszawa: Polish Academy of
Sciences Comm. of Hist. Sciences, Inst. of History, 1977.
656p., bibl. Summaries in English, French, German and
Russian.
    A country-by-country description of cultural life in the

Nazi-occupied west and east Europe. The influence of the
Reich culture on these countries is considered.

320. Poland. Ministerstwo Informacji. *The Nazi Kultur in
Poland, by several authors of necessity temporarily
anonymous*. London: H.M. Stationary Office, 1945. 220p., ill.,
maps, facsim. Published for the Polish Ministry of
Information.
   The authors were a group of persons inhabitating various
localities in German occupied Poland. Of necessity, they do
not tell us who they are, but we know from the London editors
of the book that the "authors' devoted company included
scholars of university status and international reputation,
feeling responsible for the truth of what they describe." The
book shows us the ways the Nazis wanted to destroy culture in
the occupied country.

321. Sziling, Jan. *Polityka okupanta hitlerowskiego wobec
kosciola katolickiego, 1939-1945 /The Nazi Occupant's Policy
towards the Catholic Church in the Years 1939-1945/*. Poznan:
Instytut Zachodni, 1970. 306p., bibl. (Studies on German
Occupation in Poland, vol. 11). Summary in English.
   Analysis of the policy pursued by the Nazis between 1939-45
in the Polish western regions incorporated into Germany, in
church matters. The most important elements of that policy
were: the establishment of German church administration,
anti-Polish campaigns in churches, discrimination of the
Polish language, confiscation of church property, and other
similar measures. Describes the extermination of the Polish
Catholic clergy in concentration camps. The book is based on
documents from Polish and German state and church archives.

8

CONSEQUENCES OF THE WAR

8a. BIG THREE WARTIME CONFERENCES

322. Buhite, Russell D. *Decisions at Yalta: An Appraisal of Summit Diplomacy*. Wilmington, Del.: Scholarly Resources, 1986. 156p., bibl.
University of Oklahoma's professor presents a concise account of the Yalta conference of early 1945 and a suggestive case study of general problems of summit diplomacy and of efforts to achieve detente with the Soviet Union. He analyzes the major issues that confronted the three leaders: Germany, Poland, the United Nations, the Far East, and the Declaration of Liberated Europe--considering each in a separate chapter.

323. Clemens, Diane Shaver. *Yalta*. New York: Oxford University Press, 1971. 356p., ill., portraits, maps, bibl.
Focuses on the give-and-take of the Yalta negotiations (February 1945) on the main issues: German reparations, the dismemberment of Germany, Japan, the U.N. voting formula, and the Polish question: settling western frontiers, Russian zones of influence in Poland and other European countries. Clemens observes that "... when the U.S. decided to reject its own Yalta policy following Roosevelt's death, it virtually went to war--albeit a "cold one"... Washington, not Moscow, prevented a settlement which might have left Europe intact rather than divided into blocks and camps." She favorably emphasizes Stalin's great tactical skill, and is consistently unfavorable to the U.S. Excellent bibliography.

324. De Zayas, Alfred M. *Nemesis at Potsdam: The Anglo-Americans and the Expulsion of the Germans: Background, Execution, Consequences*. 2nd ed. London; Boston: Routledge & Kegan Paul, 1977. 268p., plates, ill., bibl.
Examines in detail the concept of mass population transfers, how they came to be accepted at Potsdam and how the Allies tried to keep them "orderly and humane", in vain.

325. Eubank, Keith. *Summit at Teheran*. New York: W. Morrow, 1985. 528p., ill., map, bibl.

The first complete story of the 1943 historic meeting. It tells how it came about, why it was held in Teheran, and recounts the bitter arguments, quarrels, and secret deliberations that would change the course of history. Among the book's highlights are: planning the final strategy for the war against Hitler, the Anglo-American commitment to invade France in 1944 (Operation Overlord), and key decisions that led to Soviet domination over Poland and eastern Europe. Here Eubank contends it was at Teheran that Stalin won Anglo-American agreement on the future frontier between the Soviet Union and Poland. The Yalta conference merely ratified many of the actions taken at Teheran.

326. General Sikorski Historical Institute. *Documents on Polish-Soviet Relations, 1939-1945*. Vol. 2, *1943-1945*. Ed. Edward Raczynski and others. London: Humanities Press, 1968. 868p.

This important collection of some 400 documents on the relations between the Soviet government and Polish government-in-exile covers the period of May 1943 to August 1945, when after the resolutions of the Potsdam Conference the recognition of the Polish government in London was withdrawn by the Western Allies. It also contains much information about Allied policy in reshaping the political map of Eastern Europe.

327. Mee, Charles L. *Meeting at Potsdam*. New York: M. Evans, 1975. 370p., ill., bibl.

This is an account of the last of the Big Three wartime conferences. Meeting for two weeks in the summer 1945, Truman, Churchill and Stalin intended to finalize agreements and understandings reached earlier concerning Russia's entry into the war against Japan, the amount of German reparations, and the western border of Poland. At this point, it was agreed that Poland should occupy *temporarily* land to the east of the Oder-Neisse line. An appealing examination of the issues and major figures redrawing the map of the world.

328. Pastusiak, Longin. *Podzial i zjednoczenie Niemiec w dyplomacji Wielkiej Czworki /The Partition and Unification of Germany in the Diplomacy of the Four Great Powers/*. Katowice: Slask, 1972. 298p., ill., bibl. Summary in English and Russian.

Discusses proposals for the partition of Germany during the early post-war period as an act of punishing the perpetrators of World War II (cites certain U.S. opinions going so far as to set a scheme for sterilization of the whole German nation). Attempts to show that the plans of the partition were those of the Western powers. Concludes that the still unsolved German problem is a symptom of the confrontation of the two systems. The Polish problem shown in a broader context of "the new political deal" in the East Central Europe. Rich selection of both Polish and foreign sources.

8a1. The Polish Question

329. Churchill, Winston S. *Second World War*. Vol. 6, *Triumph and Tragedy*. Boston: Houghton Mifflin Co., 1953. 800p., maps.
This is the last of Churchill's six volumes of the history of World War II. It covers D-Day, the Teheran and Yalta conferences, the death of Roosevelt, the Potsdam conference, and others. Although Poland is one of many topics discussed in this volume, the Polish question basically preoccupies the author's thoughts. The crucial points include: forming a Polish government (Lublin vs. London); holding free elections; settling the Polish frontiers, in the east and the west; and a transfer of populations.

330. Fischer, Louis. *The Road to Yalta: Soviet Foreign Relations, 1941-1945*. New York: Harper and Row, 1972. 238p., bibl.
This well documented study surveys the wartime relations between Soviet Russia and its allies, the United States and Britain. Considerable space is devoted to Poland which the author sees as the main component of the Soviet expansionist policies and the key to Stalin's control of Europe.

331. Harper, John Lamberton, and Andrew Parlin. *The Polish Question during World War II*. Washington, D.C.: Foreign Policy Institute, Paul H. Nitze School of Advanced International Studies, Johns Hopkins University; Lanham, Md., 1990. 55p., ill., bibl. (FPI case studies, no. 15).
The purpose of this in-depth case study by the recognized scholars of the Johns Hopkins University's Foreign Policy Institute is to describe protracted negotiations conducted during World War II over the future of Poland. The negotiations involved two emotion-laden and bitterly contested issues: The location of Poland's postwar frontiers and the nature of its internal regime. This impartial account focuses on the roles of the three main parties to the dispute, the United States, Great Britain, and the Soviet Union, and, to a lesser extent, on the roles of the competing, London- and Lublin-based Polish factions. The discussion traces the development of the controversial issue, beginning with the collapse and exile of the Polish government in 1939, through the important preliminary negotiations at Teheran (1943) and Moscow (1944). It deals at length with the partial hammering out of a political formula at Yalta in early 1945 and culminates with the final negotiations that took place between February and June of the same year. The book is a valuable contribution to our knowledge of the history of the Polish question.

332. Kacewicz, George V. *Great Britain, the Soviet Union, and the Polish Goernment in Exile (1939-1945)*. The Hague; Boston: M. Nijhoff, 1979. 255p., bibl. (Studies in Contemporary History, vol. 3).
George V. Kacewicz of California State University writes with sympathy for the Polish government in exile, which can hardly be blamed for refusing to give up half of Poland without the population being consulted and without guarantees for either adequate compensation or postwar independence. He criticizes both Stalin's ruthlessness and the policy of

concessions toward him adopted first by the British and then
by the American government. The author states that no matter
what the Polish government might have done, the final outcome
could hardly have been different.

333. Konovalov, Serge, ed. *Russo-Polish Relations: An
Historical Survey*. Princeton: Princeton University Press,
1945. 110p., maps, bibl.
   The principal purpose of the survey is to report Polish-
Russian conflicts over the area east of the Curzon line and
to show the nationality composition of the 11,000,000 people
living there in 1931. Despite its somewhat pro-Russian bias,
this volume throws helpful light on a knotty problem.

334. Krzesinski, Andrew J. *Poland's Right to Justice*. New
York: Devin-Adar Co., 1946. 120p., bibl.
   The author shows the great injury done to Poland and its
consequences for the Allies and the whole world. The Yalta
decision means an unprecedented betrayal of a nation by her
allies and is contrary not only to the principle of justice
and to the Atlantic Charter but also to natural and
international laws.

335. Pastusiak, Longin. *Roosevelt a sprawa polska /Roosevelt
and the Polish Question/*. Warszawa: Ksiazka i Wiedza, 1980.
441p., plates, ill., portraits, bibl. Summary in English and
Russian.
   Based on less known or unknown papers and documents from
diplomatic archives of the U.S., Pres. Roosevelt's library,
and Library of Congress, this book by a former (in the
seventies and eighties) ambassador to the United States
provides a discussion of the Polish question in the U.S.
diplomacy, and the role it played in the relations among the
Allies, from the outbreak of the war to Roosevelt's death on
April 13, 1945. References back to the period of Munich and
up to the Potsdam conference are also made.

336. Perlmutter, Amos. *FDR and Stalin. A Not So Grand
Alliance, 1943-1945*. Columbia, Mo.: University of Missouri
Press, 1993. 331p., maps, ill., bibl.
   With the dissolution of the Soviet Union, historians are
now capable of examining the evolution of the U.S.-Soviet
relations from Moscow's perspective. Based on Soviet archival
sources as well as the materials of the Roosevelt library,
this study re-interprets the roles of Stalin and Roosevelt in
creating the Russo-American alliance, at the cost of others.
Large fragments concern the Polish question. Here Perlmutter
describes Soviet Embassy papers reporting FDR's domestic
pressures (from American Catholics and the Polish ethnic
minority, which were seen by Gromyko as the most anti-Soviet
group) that the Russians thought might impede their plans for
Poland. On this point, the author repeats known facts from
1939 to 1945 and the Yalta "sellouts".

337. Polonsky, Antony, ed. *The Great Powers and the Polish
Question 1941-1945: A Documentary Study in Cold War Origins*.
London: London School of Economics and Political Science,
1976. 282p.
   The editor's stated intention is "to let the documents

speak for themselves" and to permit "the student to make up
his own mind" upon the conflicting interpretations regarding
the policies of the Big Three towards the Polish question in
this period. For this reason he has selected 194 British
documents to which he adds a 37-p. introduction "to outline
the points of dispute rather than to make any final
judgment". The collection displays a sad story. "The British
Government and the Foreign Office retained illusions
concerning the possibility of modifying Soviet policy, but
Stalin merely waited until the success of the Red Army
changed the terms of diplomacy. The Polish government in
exile was the prisoner of the unrealistic concepts of
yester-year. What emerged was a Poland which bore little
resemblance to the old, territorially, ethnically and
politically."

338. Rozek, Edward. *Allied Wartime Diplomacy: A Pattern in
Poland*. New York: Wiley, 1958. 481p., maps, bibl.
  The book is concerned with the diplomacy of the Western
Powers and the Soviet Union relating to Poland, and of the
Polish government in the wartime years and immediately
thereafter. Discusses the composition of the Polish
government and its role. Together with the books of Lane,
Ciechanowski, and Mikolajczyk, Rozek's account is an
outstanding contribution to the study of the Polish question
during the war. Supplemented by full texts of relevant
diplomatic reports, confidential letters and official
records.

339. Shotwell, James T., and Max M. Laserson. *Poland and
Russia, 1919-1945*. New York: Carnegie Endowment for
International Peace, 1945. 114p., maps, bibl.
  A scholarly and impartial investigation of the history of
the complicated dealings between the two countries during the
period from the restoration of Poland after World War I to
1945. Texts of important documents are included. The book may
help readers understand the Polish problem.

340. Stern, Harold Peter. *The Struggle for Poland, 1941-1947*.
Washington: Public Affairs Press, 1953. 79p., maps, bibl.
  An outline of Poland's history and international relations
from Hitler's invasion in 1939 to the Soviet style elections
of 1947. The Polish question during the war with special
reference to the Soviet-Polish conflict is set out in the
context of East-West relationships. The chronology of
principal events is added in the appendix.

341. Von Riekhoff, Harald. *German-Polish Relations,
1918-1933*. Baltimore: John Hopkins Press, 1971. 421p., bibl.
  In this analysis of the diplomatic relations between the
nascent Polish and German republics, the author discusses the
clash of German revisionism in Eastern Europe with the Polish
dedication to the maintenance of the status quo in the
interwar years. Setting the dispute in its international
context, the book objectively and comprehensively handles a
centuries-old, complex and significant problem and shows the
interplay of the European diplomatic forces on the German-
Polish disagreements. The author draws heavily upon German
and Polish documentary materials.

8a2. The German Problem: The Western Territories and Resettlement

342. Buhler, Philip A. *The Oder-Neisse Line: A Reappraisal under International Law.* Boulder & New York: Distributed by Columbia University Press, 1990. 154p., maps, bibl. (East European Monographs, No. 277).
   Presents the German point of view in the dispute over the territories lost by Germany to Poland and the Soviet Union after World War Two.

343. De Zayas, Alfred M. *Nemesis at Potsdam: The Anglo-Americans and the Expulsion of the Germans: Background, Execution, Consequences.* 2nd ed. London; Boston: Routledge & Kegan Paul, 1977. 268p., plates, ill., bibl.
   Examines in detail the concept of mass population transfers, how they came to be accepted at Potsdam and how the Allies tried to keep them "orderly and humane", in vain.

344. Derlatka, Tadeusz. *Western and Northern Poland: Historical Outline, Nationality Problems, Legal Aspect, New Society, Economic Survey.* Ed. Maria Kornilowicz. Poznan: Zachodnia Agencja Prasowa, 1962. 534p., maps, bibl.
   Topics addressed in this well researched, comprehensive study are: outline history of the western territories, the expulsion of populations--Polish by Nazis during the war and German after the war, and the following socio-economic problems of the resettlement in the recovered territories. Includes sources in German with English translation.

345. Gruchman, Bohdan. *Polish Western Territories.* Translated from Polish by Wanda Libicka. Poznan: Instytut Zachodni, 1959. 267p., maps, bibl.
   The purpose of this book is to collect and elaborate the basic information concerning the Polish western territories. Avoids polemics and propaganda, trying instead to "allow figures and facts that have been confirmed and discussed many times to speak for themselves". They are used to describe demographic changes and dynamic economic development of the recovered regions.

346. Hubatsch, Walther, ed. *German Question.* Translated from German by Salvator Attanasio. New York: Herder Book Center, 1967. 511p., maps, bibl.
   Chapter entitled "The German Eastern Territories" outlines the Oder-Neisse line prior to and after the war, describes the population expulsion from the German eastern territories, and the development in these lands under "foreign administration" since 1945.

347. Jordan, Z. *Oder-Neisse Line.* London: MacNeill, 1952. 136p., maps, append.
   Prepared on the basis of the research of a Study Group set up by the Polish Freedom Movement "Independence and Democracy". This is a study of the political, economic, and European significance and implications of Poland's western frontier as the result of World War II.

348. Kaps, Johannes, ed. *The Tragedy of Silesia, 1945-46: A Documentary Account with a Special Survey of the Archdiocese of Breslau.* Translated from German. Munich: Christ Unterwegs, 1953. 576p., bibl.
   A large compilation of testimony and other documents collected by the Catholic church concerning the invasion of the Soviet troops, Polish excesses, and expulsions of the ethnic Germans in 1945 and thereafter.

349. Klafkowski, Alfons. *The Polish-German Frontier after World War II.* Translated by Edward Rothert. Poznan: Wyd. Pozn., 1972. 125p., maps, bibl.
   The coverage includes: legal foundation of the final settlement of the Polish-German frontier, Polish-German frontier as a foundation of the European territorial system, recovered territories within the organism of the Polish state, guarantees of the security of the Polish-German frontier in the system of alliances concluded by Poland, and the Potsdam agreement as a substitute for a peace treaty with Germany.

350. Kokot, Jozef. *The Logic of the Oder-Neisse Frontier.* Poznan: Wydawn. Zach., 1959. 289p., bibl.
   Approaches the problem of the postwar changes of western boundaries, as established on the Oder-Neisse line, from the standpoint of international law and deals with the demographic and economic implications of the new frontiers.

351. Lachs, Manfred. *The Polish-German Frontier: Law, Life and Logic of History.* Warszawa: Polish Scientific Publishers, 1964. 80p., bibl.
   Brief resume and defense of the new Polish western frontier.

352. Lesniewski, Andrzej, ed. *Western Frontier of Poland: Documents, Statements, Opinions.* Warsaw: Polish Institute of International Affairs; Western Press Agency, 1965. 302p.
   A selection of documents intended to provide the English-speaking reader, on the twentieth anniversary of the Potsdam Agreement, with a review of the relevant materials: legal documents, statements by both east and west European governments, and excerpts from the western press articles by journalists and scholars concerning the Oder-Neisse Line.

353. Pietrucha, Jerzy. *The Population of Western and Northern Poland.* Translated by Stanislaw Tarnowski. Warsaw: Interpress Publishers, 1972. 139p., maps, tables, charts, bibl.
   An analysis of the demographic conditions in the northern and western territories of Poland recovered from Germany after the war.

354. Rhode, Gotthold, and Wolfgang Wagner. *The Genesis of the Oder-Neisse Line in the Diplomatic Negotiations during World War II: Sources and Documents.* Stuttgart: Brentano-Verlag, 1959. 287p., bibl.
   Based on the already printed material, this is an English edition of a 1956 German-language published collection. This collection of sources is "intended to enable the reader to acquaint himself at first hand with the most important

documents and negotiations of the Second World War ...
directly connected with the genesis of the Oder-Neisse Line."
The texts of treaties, agreements, and notes are therefore
given in the original language, and in the English
translation. Detailed table of documents in chronological
arrangement. Detailed subject index. For researchers.

355. Schimitzek, Stanislaw. *Truth or Conjecture?: German
Civilian Losses in the East*. Translated from Polish. Warsaw:
Western Press Agency, 1966. 381p., ill., faxims, maps, bibl.
    Transfer of the German population from the Reich's former
eastern territory, Danzig and parts of Poland, as well as
heavy German civilian losses incurred during the tranfer are
all put in the context of political circumstances that caused
them and poor cooperation between German and Polish
officials. Abundant statistical material.

356. Schoenberg, Hans W. *Germans from the East*. The Hague: M.
Nijhoff, 1970. 366p., bibl. (Studies in Social Life series,
No. 15).
    Describes the expulsion of the ethnic Germans, their
resettlement, and subsequent groups.

357. Scholz, Albert August. *Silesia Yesterday and Today*. The
Hague: M. Nijhoff, 1964. 94p., fold map, bibl.
    A German account of the situation in Silesia in the first
years following the war: annexation of the lost territory,
transfer of German population, Russian plundering and
violations, stripping by Poles of building and other
materials and transporting them to central parts of Poland.

358. Szaz, Zolton M. *Germany's Eastern Frontiers: The Problem
of the Oder-Neisse Line*. Chicago: Henry Regnery Co., 1960.
256p., bibl.
    Covers Polish western frontiers in context of international
relations, particularly the United States and Britain versus
post-war Germany. Defines territory and people, presents
historical background, wartime, Russian role in creating the
Oder-Neisse line and German attitude.

359. Von Wiepert, Friedrich. *The Oder-Neisse Problem; towards
Fair Play in Central Europe*. Bonn: Edition Atlantic-Forum,
1964. 163p., ill., portraits, maps.
    German point of view on loss of territories to Poland.
Tries to look at this loss objectively, recognizing at the
same time that many Germans were displaced. States the
problem and then examines it in the historical perspective of
Polish-German relations through centuries.   ·

360. Wagner, Wolfgang. *The Genesis of the Oder-Neisse Line: A
Study in Diplomatic Negotiations During World War II*.
Translated from German. Stuttgart: Brentano-Verlag, 1957.
168p., maps, bibl.
    Based on primary and secondary sources, this book analyzes
the subject of the Oder-Neisse Line in the historical and
diplomatic context from the prewar period up to the Potsdam
Conference. Considers the postwar frontier consequences for
Germany and Poland. Defends a German point of view.

361. Western Press Agency. *Transfer of the German Population from Poland: Legend and Reality*. Warsaw: Western Press Agency, 1966. 54p., ill., map, bibl.
   Polish refutation of "West German propaganda" accusing Poland "of crimes committed in connection with the resettlement of the German population" from Poland.

362. Wiewiora, Boleslaw. *Polish-German Frontiers from the Standpoint of International Law*. Poznan: Wyd. Zach., 1959. 224p., bibl.
   Originally a doctoral thesis. The matters outlined regarding the frontier include: territorial changes after World War II, the Yalta and Potsdam Agreements, transfer of German population, the question of recognition of the German Democratic Republic, and the peace treaty with West Germany.

363. Wiskemann, Elizabeth. *Germany's Eastern Neighbours: Problems Relating to the Oder-Neisse and the Czech Frontier Regions*. London: Oxford University Press, 1956. 309p., maps, bibl. "Issued under the auspices of the Royal Institute of International Affairs."
   A detailed, objective discussion of developments in territories of German-Polish and German-Czech controversy in the years since Hitler's rise to power. Wiskemann analyzes the awkward, complex problems of Upper and Lower Silesia, the old "Danzig Corridor", Poznan (Posen), and the rest. Particular emphasis is given to the postwar decade, witnessing the territorial changes, expulsion of the Germans, and the new industrial activities in these lands.

8b. WAR CRIMES TRIALS

364. Cyprian, Tadeusz, and Jerzy Sawicki. *Nie oszczedzac Polski /No Mercy for Poland/*. Warszawa: Iskry, 1959. 475p., notes, portraits. Summary in English.
   The basic documentary material on war crimes committed in Poland from 1939-1945. Discusses Nazi aggression and occupation, the germanization of children, Hans Frank's diary, forced labor, public execution, and Auschwitz. Concludes with a commentary by the authors, who were prosecuting attorneys representing Poland at the Nuremberg International Military Tribunal. Epilogue reviews the last day of the trial and final statements by the accused.

365. Koehl, Robert L. *RKFDV: German Resettlement and Population Policy 1939-1945: A History of the Reich Commission for the Strengthening of Germandom*. Cambridge, Mass.: Harvard University Press, 1957. 263p., bibl. (Harvard Historical Monographs, 31).
   A well documented, thorough analysis of characteristic aspects of Nazi population policy during World War II. The author describes attempts at resettlement especially in Polish areas under German control. The study is primarily based on unpublished material collected for and used by prosecution and defense at Nuremberg in United States Trials 8 and 11. For researchers.

366. Muszkat, Marian. *Polish Charges against German War Criminals*. Warsaw: The National Office for the Investigation of German War Crimes, 1948. 232p.
Contains excerpts from 18 cases submitted to the United Nations War Crimes Committee.

367. Pilichowski, Czeslaw, ed. *Zbrodnie i sprawcy: ludobojstwo hitlerowskie przed sadem ludzkosci i historii /Nazi Crimes in the Court of Humanity and History/*. Warszawa: PWN, 1980. 943p., ill., bibl. Summaries and table of contents in English, French, and Russian.
A compilation of materials prepared by various authors for commemorating the 30th anniversary of the General Commission for Investigation of Nazi Crimes in Poland. The "publication is a review of the state of knowledge in the field of war crimes, crimes against humanity, and a review of results of prosecuting their perpetrators." A detailed problem-oriented table of contents and summaries in several languages.

368. Piotrowski, Stanislaw, ed. *Hans Frank's Diary*. Warszawa: PWN, 1961. 320p., ill., bibl.
A systematic record of the most important aspects of war crimes committed by Hans Frank while Governor General in Cracow. Based on scientific, objective, and impartial analysis of the vast amount of material included in Frank's diary and in documents brought to light at the course of the Nuremberg Trial.

8c. SOVIETIZATION

369. Davies, Norman, and Antony Polonsky, eds. *Jews in Eastern Poland and the USSR, 1939-46*. London: St. Martin's, 1991. 426p., maps, bibl. (Studies in Russia and East Europe Series).
Essays dealt with in this collection include: the role of Jews in the sovietization of Eastern Poland between 1939 and 1941; the effect of this period on Jewish response to the subsequent Nazi conquest and initiation of the "final solution"; the role Jews played in the years when the USSR reconquered the area and began to establish a communist-dominated regime in Poland; and the fate of Polish citizens of Jewish descent in the USSR. Contributors to this volume are scholars from Poland, Israel, the USSR, England, and the United States.

370. DeWeydenthal, Jan B. *The Communists of Poland: An Historical Outline*. Stanford, Calif.: Hoover Institution Press, 1978. 217p., bibl.
The book is concerned exclusively with an organized group of Communists who came to power in Poland. Concise and informative.

371. Gsovski, Vladimir, ed. *Mid-European Law Project: Church and State behind the Iron Curtain--Czechoslovakia, Hungary, Poland, Romania. With an introduction on the Soviet Union*. New York: Praeger, 1955. 311p. Free Europe Committee, Mid-European Studies Center Publications.
A depressing picture of cruel governmental efforts to

transform Churches into supporters of government policies and ultimately into Bureaus of a Socialist State.

372. Kersten, Krystyna. *The Establishment of Communist Rule in Poland, 1943-1948*. Translated by John Micgiel and Michael H. Bernhard; foreword by Jan T. Gross. Berkeley: University of California Press (Societies and culture in East-Central Europe series), 1991. 535p., ill., bibl.
This is a translation of a book by one of the country's prominent historians. Based on archival and printed materials, it describes in detail the mechanisms used by the Polish Communists supported by the Soviets, in their manipulation not only of political and military instruments but also of mass media to capture and hold political power. Extensive bibliography of primary and secondary works.

373. Kertesz, Stephen Denis, ed. *Fate of East Central Europe: Hopes and Failures of American Foreign Policy*. Notre Dame, Ind.: University of Notre Dame Press, 1956. 463p., bibl.
Chapters by 16 well-known experts on the creation of the Soviet empire in Eastern Europe and its bearing on American foreign policy. Focus on Hungary.

374. Korbonski, Andrzej. *Politics of Socialist Agriculture in Poland: 1945-1960*. New York: Columbia University Press, 1965. 330p., bibl. (East Central European Studies Columbia University Series).
Background of the political and economic position of Polish peasants in the interwar period, the struggle between the Communists and the peasants for political supremacy, beginning during the Second World War, continuing over the years of the land reform, and concluding with the defeat of the peasant political opposition in 1947. This is followed by a section in which collectivization is discussed and analyzed in various aspects. (See also Mikolajczyk).

375. Kusnierz, Bronislaw. *Stalin and the Poles: An Indictment of the Soviet Leaders*. London: Hollis and Carter, 1949. 315p., bibl.
A detailed account of what the author describes as "the crimes of Soviet imperialism." Covers period from 1939 to 1948 and describes the sovietization of Polish territory and later the postwar Polish state.

376. Lane, Arthur B. *I Saw Poland Betrayed; an American Ambassador Reports to the American People*. Indianapolis: Bobbs-Merril Co., 1948. 344p., ill., portraits, maps, bibl.
Report by the U.S. Ambassador to Poland from July 1945 to his resignation on January 19, 1947 after elections in Poland. Takes the position that Poland was abandoned to Russia by the West.

377. Mikolajczyk, Stanislaw. *Rape of Poland: Pattern of Soviet Aggression*. New York: McGraw, 1948. 309p., ill., portraits, bibl.
A heavily documented book by the first post-war Polish Prime Minister and head of the then suppressed Peasants' Party. Mikolajczyk writes that he witnessed the betrayal of Poland from every political level, and that even as the

leader of the great party he was helpless to avert the
violent destruction of the country's democratic processes and
finally had to flee in disguise. The book is a classic
exposition of the methods and aims of sovietization.

378. Monticone, Ronald C. *The Catholic Church in Communist
Poland, 1945-1985: Forty Years of Church-State Relations*.
Boulder & New York: East European Monographs (Distributed by
Columbia University Press), 1986. 227p., bibl.
   The study deals with Catholic Church-Polish government
relations from 1945 to 1985. Competently and clearly written,
this account focuses primarily on the activities of the
hierarchy, especially Cardinal Stefan Wyszynski and John Paul
II, the leaders of the government, and the activities of the
Catholic and pro-Catholic lay organizations that played a
political role, including the "Solidarity" labor union.

379. Polonsky, Antony, and Boleslaw Drukier, eds. *The
Beginnings of Comunist Rule in Poland*. London: Routledge &
Kesan Paul, 1980. 464p., plates, ill., bibl. Includes
documents translated from Polish.
   The work is concerned exclusively with the business of the
Communist movement's organs at a time when the party (PPR)
was still on the margin of power. The editors' detailed
introductory essay, glossary, list of pseudonyms, and
biographical index make this book a convenient *vade mecum*
through the intricacies of comunists' manoeuvres and
intrigues to establish control over the country.

380. Seton-Watson, Hugh. *East European Revolution*. 3rd ed.
New York: Praeger, 1956. 406p., maps, bibl.
   The purpose of this book is both to describe and analyze
the sovietization of Eastern Europe. Part 1, "Background",
covers social structure, parties and politics in Poland,
Czechoslovakia, Hungary, Bulgaria, etc. Part 2, "Axis New
Order and Resistance" leads to main topic: "Sovietization".

381. Staar, Richard Felix. *Poland, 1944-1962: The
Sovietization of a Captive People*. Baton Rouge: Louisiana
State University Press, 1962. 300p., ill., tables, maps,
bibl.
   This study is concerned with the beginnings of the
sovietization of Polish life and the Communist system's
structure. A product of extensive research, the book relies
mainly on official sources and is rich in tables, maps,
diagrams and detail. The study's important contribution is
its analysis of the social composition of the Polish ruling
party, its leadership, the policies and the pressure groups
within the party.

382. Strong, Anna Louise (Mrs Joel Shubin). *I Saw the New
Poland*. Boston: Little, Brown & Co., 1946. 280p.
   An interesting, and in places even moving account of the
life in Poland during concluding stages of the war as it
appeared to this American correspondent. One feels that the
author has a genuine sympathy for the Polish people and their
determination to rebuild their country from ruins. However,
Strong's well-known identity with propagandistic Moscow
journalism and her pro-Soviet bias cause that the book fails

to be an objective document. She sides with the Lublin
government rather than with the Polish government in London.

383. Toranska, Teresa. *"Them": Stalin's Polish Puppets*.
Translated from Polish By A. Kolakowska. 1st U.S. ed. New
York: Harper & Row, 1987. 384p., portraits.
   A record of interviews by a journalist with five high
officials of postwar Poland. The Solidarity period enabled
her to shed fresh light on the politics of the post-1945 era.
Berman, Ochab, Staszewski, Werfel, and Julia Minc, all prewar
communists, were sent to Poland by Stalin to help build his
new order, Soviet style. There would be no relationships with
London Poles, nationalists, no free elections, or any other
"Western notions". Squadrons of Soviet advisers and officials
came too.

384. Zajdlerowa, Zoe. *The Dark Side of the Moon*. London:
Faber, 1946. 299p.
   An account of Polish-Soviet relations from 1939 to 1945
from the standpoint of Soviet actions as a result of the 1939
pact between Germany and the Soviet Union and the subsequent
Soviet occupation of the eastern part of Poland. Describes
the imposition of the Soviet pattern of life upon the Poles
and the resultant consequences.

385. _____ . *The Dark Side of the Moon: A New Edition*. Ed.
by J. Coutouvidis and Thomas Lane. London: Harvester
Wheatsheaf, 1989. 182p., ill., maps, bibl.
   The work reissued on the fiftieth anniversary of the
invasion of Poland by Nazi Germany and the Soviet Union. One
of the editors' objectives in preparing this new, second
edition was "to make it available to a new generation of
general readers at a time of intense Western interest in
political developments in Eastern Europe and the Soviet
Union" (p ix) following the Gorbachev *perestroika*.

8d. COLD WAR

386. Anderson, Sheldon R. *A Dollar to Poland Is a Dollar to
Russia: U.S. Economic Policy toward Poland, 1945-1952*. New
York: Garland Publishing, 1993. 242p., bibl. (Foreign
Economic Policy of the Unted States series). Originally
presented as the author's Ph.D. thesis.
   Unlike the Soviets, Poland sought to increase its
commercial contacts with the West after the war. But by 1947,
most U.S. government officials assumed that the Soviets had a
full-fledged satellite relationship with Poland. The author
challenges this view. In this study of postwar Polish and
American diplomacy, he analyzes the objectives and actions of
Poland's diplomacy in this direction and shows how these
efforts influenced American foreign policy. Anderson attempts
to convey a balanced and realistic account of the early Cold
War period as well as to present a clearer picture of Soviet
economic policy toward Poland.

387. Davis, Lynn Etheridge. *The Cold War Begins: Soviet-
American Conflict over Eastern Europe*. Princeton, NJ:
Princeton University Press, 1974. 427p., bibl.

A discussion over who started the Cold War. The author
offers a thorough and scholarly argument in favor of
"acquitting" the U.S. First she explores the situation as it
existed in Eastern Europe in 1942; then she examines the
U.S.-Soviet Union problem and the following confrontations in
Poland, Rumania, Hungary, Bulgaria, Yugoslavia and
Czechoslovakia. The discussion on Poland, which many consider
the central starting point of the Cold War, is particularly
strong and well balanced. Also included is a review of the
Yalta and Potsdam conferences. Extensive use of state
sources.

388. Gaddis, John Lewis. *The United States and the Origins of
the Cold War, 1941-1947*. New York: Columbia University Press,
1972. 396p., bibl. (Contemporary American history series).
   This study seeks to analyze a number of determinants that
affected the U.S.-Soviet relations during and immediately
after World War II: economic assistance, Germany, Soviet
domination over Poland, and other East European countries,
the A-bomb, and international communism. Concludes that the
U.S. was less responsible than the U.S.S.R. for the growing
tensions between them.

389. Kertesz, Stephen Denis, ed. *Fate of East Central Europe:
Hopes and Failures of American Foreign Policy*. Notre Dame,
Ind.: University of Notre Dame Press, 1956. 463p., bibl.
   Chapters by 16 well-known experts on the creation of the
Soviet empire in Eastern Europe and its bearing on American
foreign policy. Focus on Hungary.

390. Lukas, Richard C. *Bitter Legacy: Polish-American
Relations in the Wake of World War II*. Lexington, Ky:
University Press of Kentucky, 1982. 191p., bibl.
   An interesting and challenging analysis of Polish-American
relations from the Potsdam Conference through the forged
elections in Poland, 1947. Lukas seeks to show many factors
which made American policy unable to reverse the process
begun at the Yalta Conference that transformed Poland into a
communist state. He argues, for instance, that largely
through economic diplomacy, the United States expected to
influence the Polish situation. The author suggests that such
a policy was unrealistic.

391. Mastny, Vojtech. *Russia's Road to the Cold War:
Diplomacy, Warfare, and the Politics of Communism, 1941-1945*.
New York: Columbia University Press, 1979. 409p., bibl.
   Focus on Soviet policy in the years between the Nazi
invasion of 1941 and the Potsdam Conference of 1945. The
author seeks to show how Stalin's humiliation at the German
aggression reinforced his cynical opportunism and his desire
for Soviet control of Poland and other East European
countries. While Mastny does not discover new ground with
regard to Poland, he offers his own interpretations of some
questions, including, for example, the Soviet attitudes
toward European resistance movements, or the way Stalin
helped to crush the Warsaw uprising.

392. Poland. Ministerstwo Spraw Zagranicznych. *Documents on the Hostile Policy of the United States Government towards People's Poland*. Warsaw: Ministry of Foreign Affairs, 1953. 245p., ill., facsims.
   A selection of documents issued by the U.S. and Polish officials in the years of 1945-1953. They are intended to illustrate "the hostile policy of the United States Government towards People's Poland". They are also to serve as "an indictment against the United States on the charge of conspiracy against the territorial integrity and the independence of the Polish People's Republic." Foreword written in a typical communist jargon. Drawn from the archives of the Ministry of Foreign Affairs. For researchers.

393. Snow, Edgar. *Pattern of Soviet Power*. New York: Random House, 1945. 219p., plates, portraits.
   Outlines some of the Soviet regime's attitudes and aspirations in international politics, particularly on such questions as the program for Poland, Germany, the Balkans, and the Mongolian frontier. Other issues discussed include Russia's relations with Taiwan and the possibility of her entry into the war with Japan.

394. Wilmot, Chester. *Struggle for Europe*. New York: Harper, 1952. 766p., ill., maps, bibl.
   Based on a wide body of source material, this book traces the main events of Anglo-American operations in Western Europe up to the German surrender, and then comes to the political problems of Europe. In this section Wilmot offers a well-founded series of explanations of how Russia came to dominate the post-war scene both in East Europe and Asia (China, Korea), how and why the Western Allies, while gaining military victory, suffered political defeat.

9
POST-WAR PERIOD

9a. GENERAL ACCOUNTS

395. Barnett, Clifford R. *Poland: Its People, Its Society, Its Culture*. New Haven, Conn.: HRAF Press, 1958. 470p., maps, bibl. (Survey of world cultures).
   The survey looks briefly at Poland's past but concentrates on the twentieth century, especially on the post-war period. The material is grouped under such headings as geography and population, religions, political system, government structure and the role of the Communist party, domestic and foreign trade, ethnic groups and languages, and art and intellectual expression.

396. Kulski, Wladyslaw W. *Germany and Poland: From War to Peaceful Relations*. Syracuse: Syracuse University Press, 1976. 336p., bibl.
   An analysis of both the Polish and German points of view regarding their mutual relations during the pre- and post-war periods. It also covers West German-Polish relations through the 1970s. The author places these relations in the broader context of Europe's security issues, East-West detente, and German reunification.

397. Rachwald, Arthur R. *Poland between the Superpowers: Security vs. Economic Recovery*. Boulder, Colo.: Westview Press, 1983. 154p., bibl.
   Examines Poland's foreign and domestic policies since World War II in light of the country's relations with the Soviet Union and the West, especially the United States. The author's thesis: centuries of pillage and dismemberment by foreign powers left Poland with one overriding goal: security and territorial integrity, including recognition of the Oder-Neisse border. Seeks to demonstrate that Poland's rulers have pursued this goal at the expense of all else, including "the domestic system preferred by most Poles," and the economic prosperity that could have resulted from closer ties with the West.

398. Woods, William. *Poland: Eagle in the East: A Survey of
Modern Times.* New York: Hill & Wang, 1968. 272p., plates,
bibl.
  A panorama of postwar Poland. The book opens with a
discussion of World War II in Poland, the underground, the
Warsaw Ghetto uprising, the death camps, the Battle of
Warsaw, and moves on to the postwar recovery in industry and
farming, the resurgence of the arts and literature, the
postwar political scene, the Communist Party, the Catholic
Church, and Polish attitudes toward Russia and Germany. The
author's "account of the relations between Poles and Jews
before, during, and after the occupation makes a great effort
to be fair in a field where others take leave of their
senses." (Neal Ascherson, *NY Rev of Books* 12:27 May 8, '69).

9b. SOCIAL, POLITICAL, AND ECONOMIC HISTORY

399. Adam, Jan. *Employment and Wage Policies in Poland,
Czechoslovakia, and Hungary since 1950.* New York: St.
Martin's Press, 1984. 251p., bibl.
  Presents a clear account of wage regulation in the three
countries, and of its collapse in Poland in 1980. Concludes
that the commitment to full employment and the pressures to
restrict income differentials set up obstacles to the
implementation of economic reforms of the market type.
Altogether, this book provides a useful corrective to the
view that in a one-party state with no free trade union,
control over labor and wages is a simple matter.

400. Alton, Thad Paul. *Polish Postwar Economy.* New York:
Columbia University Press, 1955. 330p., tables, bibl.
(Studies of the Russian Institute, Columbia University).
  A study of the Russian Institute of Columbia University on
Polish economic planning and development under the Communist
regime. As in other areas of the Soviet orbit, marked
advances in industry have been accompanied by difficulties in
agriculture and a failure to bring about improvement in
living standards. Although essentially a compilation of
Polish official statistical and legal material on the postwar
economy, the book is a valuable reference work.

401. Aslund, Anders. *Private Enterprise in Eastern Europe:
The Non-Agricultural Private Sector in Poland and the GDR,
1945-1983.* Foreword by Wlodzimierz Brus. New York: St.
Martin's Press, 1985. 294p., bibl. Based on doctoral
thesis--St. Anthony's College, Oxford, 1982.
  This study of legal private enterprise (outside
agriculture) in the two socialist countries is based on
official statistics, party documents, Polish and both East
and West German publications, and personal interviews in
Poland and the GDR.

402. Coutouvidis, John, and Jaime Reynolds. *Poland,
1939-1947.* Leicester, UK: Leicester University Press, 1986.
393p., plates, ill., maps, bibl. (Politics of Liberation
Series).
  Based in part on the dissertation of one of the authors,
this study concentrates on Poland's politics, government, and

ruling circles of the pre- and post-war period. For the
period 1939-44, the authors' attention is focused on the
relationship between Churchill's and Sikorski's governments.
The second half gives a good picture of the intensity of the
struggle for power between the parties and individuals
forming the postwar coalition government.

403. Griffith, William E., ed. *Central and Eastern Europe:
The Opening Curtain?* Boulder, Colo: Westview Press, 1989.
458p., ill., bibl.
   The collection offers comparative articles, country studies
and contributions by the Western leading observers on a wide
range of topics, from economics and trade to human rights and
socio-economic organization in Central and Eastern Europe.
The volume attempts to portray the postwar dramatic period in
this region's political history. Clear-cut country studies
include Poland, Czechoslovakia, Hungary and Yugoslavia.

404. Korbonski, Andrzej. *Politics of Socialist Agriculture in
Poland: 1945-1960.* New York: Columbia University Press, 1965.
330p., bibl. (East Central European Studies Columbia
University series).
   Background of the political and economic position of Polish
peasants in the interwar period, the struggle between the
Communists and the peasants for political supremacy,
beginning during the Second World War, continuing over the
years of the land reform, and concluding with the defeat of
the peasant political opposition in 1947. This is followed by
a section in which collectivization is discussed and analyzed
in various aspects. (See also Mikolajczyk).

405. Kruszewski, Z. Anthony. *The Oder-Neisse Boundary and
Poland's Modernization: The Socioeconomic and Political
Impact. Foreword by Morton A. Kaplan.* New York: Praeger,
1972. 245p., maps, bibl.
   The main point of Dr. Kruszewski's study is that the
acquisition of the territories east of the Oder-Neisse was
the determining factor for Poland's modernization and
economic advance after World War II, due to the shift of
resource and manpower base. Deals with population migrations
and the fluctuating economic structure of the region.
Numerous statistical data, bibliographic sources (mostly
Polish), the appendix including the treaty between Poland and
German Democratic Republic, as well as between Poland and
Federal Republic of Germany add to the value of this volume.

406. Michta, Andrew A. *Red Eagle: The Army in Polish
Politics, 1944-1988.* Stanford, Calif.: Hoover Institution
Press, 1990. 270p., bibl. (Hoover Press Publ., 386).
   The study traces the evolution of Polish army's involvement
in the country's domestic affairs since WW II and analyzes
the course of events that brought General Wojciech Jaruzelski
and the military to center stage in Poland's political drama
following the 1981 dissolution of Solidarity and imposition
of martial law.

407. Monticone, Ronald C. *The Catholic Church in Communist
Poland, 1945-1985: Forty Years of Church-State Relations.*
Boulder & New York: East European Monographs (Distributed by

Columbia University Press), 1986. 227p., bibl.
   The study deals with Catholic Church-Polish government
relations from 1945 to 1985. Competently and clearly written,
this account focuses primarily on the activities of the
hierarchy, especially Cardinal Stefan Wyszynski and John Paul
II, the leaders of the government, and the activities of the
Catholic and pro-Catholic lay organizations that played a
political role, including the "Solidarity" labor union.

408. Shen, Raphael. *The Polish Economy: Legacies from the
Past, Prospects for the Future*. New York: Praeger, 1992.
226p., ill., bibl.
   In this study of Polish economic reforms since the 1950s,
the author (University of Detroit) argues for a process of
"gradualism" rather than "shock therapy" in transforming the
Soviet-style managed economy into a market system. The book
is more descriptive than analytical. Useful as a supplemental
source and an alternative view on economic systems and
transitions occurring in socialist economies.

AUTHOR INDEX

TITLE INDEX

SUBJECT INDEX

See also Big Three wartime
  conferences
Truman, Harry S., 327

Ultra. See S.O.E.
United Nations, 322-23

V-weapons, 123, 167
Von dem Bach, Erich, 261

War
  chronology of military
    events, 107, 127
  chronology of political
    events, 107, 127,
  history (general), 106-07,
    109, 111
War crimes and criminals, 227,
  261-66, 268
War crimes trials, 227, 265-
  66, 268, 303, 365-67
War origins and outbreak
  (general), 19, 24, 42, 45,
  53-54, 69-72, 74, 76, 79-80,
  82-84, 86
  See also Danzig; Hitler-

Stalin Pact; Silesia
Warsaw ghetto (general), 180,
  270-74, 276, 281, 283,
  287-88
  Jewish Fighting
    Organization, 276, 279
  uprising (1943), 157, 270,
    279, 282, 285, 288-89
  See also Jewish ghettos
Warsaw uprising (1944), 158-65
  and Soviet policy toward,
    115, 156, 163-65, 391
Wartime Polish government. See
  Polish government-in-exile
Wawel Royal Castle, art
  treasures, 315
West Germany. See Foreign
  relations, GFR-

Yalta conference (1945), 28,
  189, 196, 213, 322-23, 329-
  31, 334, 362
  See also Big Three wartime
    conferences
Yeltsin, B, 291

About the Author

WALTER OKONSKI is a bibliographer at LS, Inc., New York, where he is responsible for bibliographic processing of documents in English and East European languages. He received degrees in library science from the University of Wroclaw, Poland, and the Graduate School of Library and Information Studies at the City University of New York.

www.ingramcontent.com/pod-product-compliance
Lightning Source LLC
Chambersburg PA
CBHW020359100426
42812CB00001B/118